Celebrating Festivals
Around the World

Evelyn Francis Capel

First edition 1991

© Evelyn Francis Capel, 1991

Cover design: S. Gulbekian (with thanks to Margaret Shillan for use of sun motif)

A catalogue record for this book is available from the British Library

ISBN 0 904693 29 5

Typeset by DP Photosetting, Aylesbury, Bucks
Printed in Great Britain

Contents

Foreword

The purpose of this book is to explore the question of what it means in real life that the Christian year is an experience in common in the northern and southern parts of the world, even though the changes of the seasons are experienced the other way round. Practical problems arise from the fact that Christmas, which falls at midwinter in the North, inevitably faces the people in the South at midsummer. The Christian festivals have all emerged in the developing history of Christianity in the North. What happens therefore in the South? Are the festivals of the Christian year tied to the seasons, or should they be held in common, regardless of nature, all the world over?

The purpose of the following pages is to consider this problem. In so doing, in realizing that Christianity was brought into the world by Christ for everyone throughout the world, regardless of circumstances, it becomes clear that the festivals of the Christian year are not regulated by the seasons. They bring the experience of what the coming of Christ from the heavens to the Earth produces in history for everyone. The festivals are not products of nature, they are inserted into life on Earth from the worlds of the heavens. It is their purpose to show the human soul that the spirit of man is of heavenly origin, but becomes conscious of itself in the circumstances of the Earth. Being human, we are not of nature, but are inserted into it. Christ is an independent Being of the heavens, changing the history of mankind by His arrival in this world. From this point of view, the beings who work in nature are active in their own way, producing the rhythm of the natural year. They can be recognized in their own sphere of existence. The Christ, known to the earliest Christians in the Celtic regions as the King of the Sun, produces the spiritual rhythm of the year for the whole Earth. It is not in experience difficult to unite the natural rhythm of the year with the spiritual one as might be expected by someone who has never lived with it. Christ is the helper and healer of all mankind for the sake of the future. In nature, He is the King of the Sun who shines for the whole Earth.

1

Celebrating Festivals

Four seasons, winter, spring, summer, autumn, make up the rhythm of the Earth's year. Those who live close to nature notice the effects of the seasons more, while those at home in the cities may notice this rhythm less. But it is still a fact of life. Towards the centre of the Earth, in the tropical regions, the changes are less obvious. In the southern hemisphere, it is less clear that the weather follows the seasons than it is in the North, where the character of the season goes hand in hand with the type of weather. In modern life, technology tends to take over and through its remarkable inventions relieves people from the pressures of nature. Nowadays, it is no longer natural to go to sleep when the daylight disappears and to awaken at dawn. People live as much with systems of lighting as they do with the procession of light following darkness and darkness following light. Lighting systems are followed by heating arrangements, liberating social life from the rhythms of nature.

In our habits of living, the liberating influences of technology are a matter of course. Our habits are not bound to the movements of Sun, Moon and stars. Although this is so, we live in another connection with their influences. What we see shining in the sky is, in another sense, a series of temples for the heavenly beings who inhabit them. There is an especial lore about these beings who are called, by tradition, the Hierarchies. They wield in the world the forces which are experienced by us as influences at work in our own human nature. They reveal themselves in the work they do, but their origin is mostly unrecognized at the present time. Those who are encountered in the natural rhythm of the year are given the title, even today, of Archangels. Well known in the experience of people are those that work in the personal destiny or capacities of individual persons. They are the Angels. The Archangels are above them in rank, and even among these there are individual differences, known through the type of work they are able to undertake. Archangels lead people in groups. The more advanced ones will influence the group to which everyone belongs according to his own generation. As the generations follow one another, history is being made. As the seasons of the year follow each other, so are certain experiences discovered by those who are living on Earth together at the same time in history. Certain Archangels have evolved so far that they can share in caring, each in his own way, for the evolution of mankind. Because they live so near to man, they are, by old tradition, recognized by their effects and named accordingly by those who are receptive to them. Their names can be recited: Gabriel, Raphael, Uriel, and Michael. The names were given to them by the Hebrews but can still be used now.

They are beings who move through time. They can be imagined as dancers, as eurythmists, setting patterns through their movements that inspire the rising and falling of the seasons of the year. The patterns change, yet nevertheless they remain the same. The spring comes and passes into summer, moving on towards winter. They become familiar, and are expected to return just as they fade. Nevertheless, if one looks back over a number of years, it is noticeable that no two springs have in fact been the same in one's experience. The last season can be compared with the one before, and the one before that, and they will seem to be very varied. And yet we can say that we have seen the spring. Even in terms of modern methods of measurement, from which statistics are made, it is still really so that each season has a character of its own, but how much beyond calculation are the variations from season to season. There is a pattern that is never the same. What amazing feats of imagination can the Archangels perform.

Furthermore, the Archangels are on the move. Their path goes from one side of the Earth to the other, from North to South. With all the variations which are noticeable between the northern and southern hemispheres, the characteristics of the four seasons are still to be recognized. The organization of human activities still follows the pattern. The living body of the Earth is clothed with the beauties that the dance of the seasons can provide. They are in constant change and our experiences move with them. In the region of matter, there is a certain permanence, but the seasons are in movement, the Archangels dance, and human hearts move with them. Not only do the four great Archangels of the year have names, but they have characters. They have spiritual influences that shine upon those who share the pattern of the dance.

The Archangel Gabriel cares for the descent of heavenly influences into the earthly world. He is in one sense a loving, caring character, who brings into the life of the human soul that which makes us aware that we have been born out of the heavens into the Earth. He is, by old custom, the Archangel of annunciation. He prepares and announces the promise, and watches over its fulfilment. He reminds those who live on the Earth of the mysteries of birth. All human souls have come from somewhere outside the Earth. They are prepared for the descent into a different kind of world.

They must be led, cared for and directed. The Archangel is a messenger of the heavenly past. He does not bring that which stays forever, but is a reminder of that which will take us back to whence we came. The little space on Earth will not always hold us, for human souls are drawn back as much as they are drawn onwards. They must care for the harvest with which they should return, as much as the seed which was planted at the beginning. The heavenly propensities in human character are under the care of this Archangel. They shine in beauty on the Earth, just as much as the plants bring the essence of their beauty into Earth existence and then withdraw it again for it to be renewed in the place of its origin. Gabriel is the Archangel who comes out of the heavens into the Earth, brings us joy and then must take it back and keep us waiting in expectation of the return.

Among the four Gospels, that of St Luke especially tells the tale of Gabriel. How often have the joys he brings been represented in art. Both before and after the coming of the Christ Child has the mystery of the descent from heaven been proclaimed under the protection of Gabriel. In the Gospel of St Luke, the watchers in the night are described receiving the annunciation of His coming. They are the shepherds who have the task of protecting their sheep against the dangers that come by night. All the others, who were behaving correctly as citizens should do, were asleep in their beds. If they knew that the Angels were singing, it was in their dreams. But those who were awake heard the voices of the Angels and saw their light when the door between Earth and heaven was opened. They responded at once to the opening of the door of heaven and, as soon as circumstances allowed, they stood in the stable with Mary and Joseph beside the Christ Child. They responded with joy to the annunciation of His coming.

In the Gospel of St Matthew, there is quite another story. The Wise Men in the East had learnt to read the kind of writing which moving stars make in the sky. They likewise received the annunciation of His coming. The Archangel who led them was also Gabriel and they had to make a long and difficult journey from their earthly homes until they could find the meaning of that which they had learnt from the script of the stars. They knew what the stars had told them, but they had to seek until they found the heavenly counterpart on Earth. As they did so, they were forced to learn what the Angel of the annunciation had not told them, that powers reigned here on the Earth who rejected that which came from the heavens. The Three Wise Men had to encounter Herod. They had no means in their own intelligence of either understanding or dealing with the danger. But the Archangel who called them had to instruct them how to protect that which came from the heavens under the conditions on Earth. They were saved from losing what they came to worship by the wisdom of the Archangel. He directed their ways as he did likewise those of the Child's parents. The Kings went back to the homes they knew, but the Child was taken to an unknown land. His companions, according to the old pictures, were the souls of the little children who had been killed for His sake at the command of the enemy on Earth, Herod, the king in this world. The heavenly Child had companions from Heaven and was protected by the Archangel, whose character it is to bring what is heavenly into this world of the Earth.

The Archangel is renowned in many legends and many pictures that have emerged from the early portions of the Gospels of St Luke and St Matthew. By common consent, he is depicted holding the symbol of the lily. In every sense this flower is rightfully his. All flowers that grow from bulbs are true to their heavenly origin and less dependent than other plants on earthly conditions and weather. They proclaim the triumph of heavenly forces on Earth. The first flowers in the cold of a northern winter are the delicate snowdrops. They are quite undemanding and they survive of themselves. Other winter-flowering plants are to be found and they are the true decoration for the season of Gabriel. They have gentle qualities, not known to the flowers of the summer, and yet they have the strongest power of endurance. In the southern hemisphere, where the impact of summer can be too strong for many flowers, the most beautiful blossoms tend to appear in the wintertime of Gabriel. At the same time, a wonderful variety of blossoms related to the lily are to be found. In the North, one might say, Gabriel must carry his lily. In the South, he will walk in a garden of lilies.

The Archangel Raphael is devoted to caring for the influences of healing. Today, when the attitude to sickness and suffering is often the attempt to get rid of it, healing remains a great mystery. Raphael guards for the human soul the power to transform, to bring good out of woe. In the present time, it is sometimes difficult to understand that the woes of sickness and suffering have their own value when the power to transform them is recognized. Illness can be thought of as a waste of time, carrying the threat of what will be missed and left out of the flow of experience going on around us. Mothers are sometimes reproached for allowing their children to fall ill. Adults absent from their job, meeting or undertaking, incur the same reproach. Illness is a hindrance that should not be tolerated. The Archangel Raphael throws a different light upon it. He carries the staff of the two snakes, one moving downwards, the other upwards. He is the guardian of the forces beyond ourselves that work for the balance of health.

It is only human to wish to avoid sickness and suffering. But from another point of view—one that calls the spiritual forces into daily life—a higher purpose can be detected in illness. The process of healing is one of transformation. A sick person healed is someone born again with new forces. He has not just lost the hindrance and the pain; he has been renewed and fitted out again with fresh forces. If he can start to observe himself, he will find that his mind is refreshed, that new ideas appeal to him differently, that his relationship with his own character has been transformed. The person is not so much renewed as reborn. So it comes about that Raphael is naturally the Archangel of springtime. Much is lost in the dark of winter that is born again in the growing light of the spring.

In the autumn the leaves lose their green, turn the colour of flames in a fire, fall off and are gone. They come back again renewed in the strength of the spring. They are healed by being lost and allowed to be born again. People do not necessarily feel stronger in the spring than in the winter. This can only be truly said of plants. People differ from one another in their constitution, one season or the other being more suitable for them. But that which brings about renewal of itself is the strength that provides healing. What is health but the continual overcoming of falling sick and starting again? One cannot say that illness is a hindrance. One can look instead at all that happens because one is able to be ill and be born again in health. That which comes from above lifts us up from that which has cast us down. The movement of the one snake answers the movement of the other on the staff of Mercury, which has become the sign of the Archangel Raphael. The forces from below draw the human soul down into the experience of decay. That which comes from the grace of Raphael from above lifts up our being with the strength of renewal.

Any adverse experience teaches the soul that the powers of destruction have gripped the human constitution; in a sense the soul is reminded that the fallen nature of man continues to be at work. The force of death has its grip on the one who lives in a human body, but that which works from above through the cosmic strength of the universe gives to the human soul the strength to survive the grip of the deadening forces and to be renewed in the power of the light that lifts up as the forces of death pull down. What does it mean when one person says to another, 'How are you?' It is customary to answer politely, 'I am all right.' It would be more accurate to say, 'The balance is being held in me; I have not yet gone under.' How odd it would sound, according to our conventions, but how real in the presence of the Archangel. Because he continues to surround us with his activity, we experience more than the destructive part of our nature. The uplifting part is revealed in the wisdom that continually streams into man on earth from the heights which dispense life and light. The darkness is known to our souls because in the midst of life we are in death. The light from above continually lifts up our hearts. The working of the Archangel Raphael sheds the grace of this experience into our hearts. Just as, without the work of Gabriel, the process by which the heavenly forces enter the world would be lost, so through the Archangel Raphael the healing from the heavens above reaches us to penetrate our human nature with which we exist.

What then is owed in our existence to the Archangel Uriel? He is manifested in the season of summer, when light and warmth envelops us. The powers of growth in the world are transformed into the powers of ripening. The cold earth becomes warm and fruitful. The Archangel says to mankind: 'What has become of you? You came to Earth like a seed being planted. Your soul is at risk between that which comes from below and that which comes from above. You emerge through the wisdom that allows you to distinguish between good and evil. You have the will to act, to bring the fruits of good and evil from within yourself. The good that you can speak and can do rises up to the heavens, from which the light comes. The evil that you think and do drops down into the darkness below. You lift your being up in goodness. You throw it down when you tolerate your ability to do wrong. You have been placed in the world between the light and the dark, between the good and the evil. You have been created by the power of God. You now begin to create yourself between the good and evil. Watch for your harvest. Choose what will become of it. Know that you have the power over what you produce.'

Once upon a time in the past, it was said of the Archangel Uriel that he will preside over the Last Judgment. Nowadays, it can be said that he is already presiding over the judgment that a person makes over himself. He gathers the creative forces of the good which a human soul can use and they are absorbed into our heavenly history. He lets accumulate the waste of evil as the world rubbish below and the question arises, how shall the rubbish be disposed of. What will become of it?

Nevertheless, Uriel holds in front of the human soul the picture of his creation, of man intended for the good, meant to become and remain the child of God, who fulfils his godhead in thinking and doing, blest and inspired by the light. How often can one say of another human being, out of pity, 'poor thing'? But he was never intended to become a poor thing, but to be the one who brings the heavenly life down to the Earth and makes of himself a child of God in a god-forsaken world. Man is not god-forsaken, he is god-endowed and he himself should endow the world with godliness. The Archangel Uriel continues to hold the heavenly ideal of man before the eyes of our hearts. Are you like this? Do you behave like this, or have you forgotten from whence you came? Are you willing to walk with God outside the Garden of Paradise, as you once walked in it? In all these questions, judgment is implied. The human soul reflects upon itself. The question is put to us from the heights, that we may question ourselves from the depths. We are answerable to our Creator when He calls from the heights of Light, but we are answerable to ourselves when we see the light in the darkness.

The Archangel Michael holds the sword of courage. His forces pour into the human heart, just when the vision set out by Uriel could overwhelm the individual person with the sense of his responsibilities. Uriel's picture of what it means to be human may uplift the heart, but it presents the problem of how human life on Earth can be lived in response to it. The Dragon can snarl at us, and he can also laugh, that beings burdened with so much weakness can expect to become heroes. The Archangel Michael does not descend into incarnation on the Earth, but he reaches up into the world of the stars and fetches down sparks of the courage out of which the world was created by God. He sends sparks of fire into human hearts that know the dark burden of fear. It would be dangerous if people did not know how to be afraid. They would not be able to call up the powers of will that deeds require. Their actions would become happy-go-lucky; they would not develop a sense of responsibility through which to take part in the divine decision to create. Among the fairy-tales of Grimm there is one about the prince who was afraid of nothing. He's not represented as a hero because of this, but rather as a kind of nincompoop. The story is about all the efforts made to teach him the experience of fear. Without knowing it and calling up courage to deal with it, he cannot truly be a prince. Fear belongs to the life on Earth. Courage descends from the divine world.

In this sense, it is a true picture of the Archangel that he holds his sword, and that sparks of courage descend from the sphere of the stars into the hearts of people. His season is the autumn when, as the brightness of summer fades, the light of understanding is allowed to become stronger in the human mind. He presides over the process through which inner activity strengthens as the life in the world around us weakens. Man is no longer a creature of the world around, when the creative courage lightens within him. People begin to live less from what is provided by nature and more from what depends upon themselves. That which distinguishes Michael is devotion to the deed of Christ done upon the Earth. There has developed in his heart in the course of time the mission to share his understanding with human souls. Out of his devotion to the divine world, he has given us the courage to withstand the attacks of Evil. He develops in our own time, out of his great devotion to Christ, greater divine wisdom and understanding. It is directed towards that Mystery of human history, which is the greatest. He is filled with the inspiration flowing to him from the deed of Christ, who descended with intent from the heights of Heaven to the depths of Earth and performed the deed on Golgotha. As the Archangel has grown and developed his understanding of the work of Christ, so he gives to mankind the power of its spiritual imagination to enter into that which he knows. To the gift of courage he adds the gift of insight.

More than the other Archangels, he shares the dilemma of being human. Cast out into the world, where he has to face the Devil in his own right, man is confronted with more than he knows how to accomplish. But the Archangel who once overcame the Dragon in the heavens now shares in the fight on Earth. Christ, who has descended from the heavens to the Earth to take the fate of mankind into His own history, has not left man alone, but has joined him. The Archangel who most of all serves Christ comes to the help of man. Michael's faith in mankind is illumined by his faith in Christ. The Resurrection of Christ is to be shared with man. In the future man is to become the one who resurrects and he will carry the knowledge of this mystery up into the heavens, from whence he came. Michael guards that which inspires and fosters the continuing process of the resurrection of man. He still wards off the Dragon, who wishes to consume the mystery himself. His gift of courage streams likewise into the future. That which can protect the human soul from the fear of being consumed is the power that will make possible not just the overcoming of the Dragon but the transformation of him. The Dragon will need to be redeemed, but he will not be able to bring this about himself. The courage in the hearts of people, their devotion to the Mystery of Resurrection, will work into the nature of the Dragon himself. Evil will be subject to metamorphosis. It will be changed into that power which in the time to come will serve the Christ. The courage to withstand will become the courage to transform. This comes into human history as the gift of Michael to human hearts.

2

The Working of Archangels

Archangels are spiritual beings on the move, performing ritual dances round the Earth. They move in the course of the seasons, augmenting with their spiritual activity the rhythms of nature. They are in harmony with the Earth itself. The living, moving character of the Earth is manifested in relationship to the heavens above. The continuing conversation between what comes from above and what rises from below makes the course of the seasons. They move in time and in space. The Earth has two halves, above and below, meeting in the centre at the line described mathematically as the equator. To cross the equator is to find oneself in the other half of the Earth, where everything is the reverse of what was found in the half that one has left. The seasons are back to front: summer in the North brings winter in the South; spring in the South brings autumn in the North. The year's rhythm of time brings about the opposite reflection in space; at the centre, the equator, the seasonal changes are slight.

That which the Archangels can perform from the North is distinct from that which they can give from the South. When the Archangel works down from above, he inspires the human mind. Thoughts and experiences shine into the inner life as the character of the Archangel brings them to life. When, from the point of view of the North, the Archangel works from below, when the inspiration streams through the Earth itself, his forces flow directly into the human constitution of those who are inhabiting the Earth's northern half. Naturally, for those inhabiting the South, when the Archangel is in the North, his spiritual forces will work through the Earth into the constitutions of those who dwell in the South. Whenever an Archangel sends his forces from above, they become inspiration to the souls of those living on that side of the Earth and for those on the other side, where the forces must pass first through the Earth, they work into the bodily constitution to harmonize and heal it. The same Archangel can inspire thoughts and feelings when he is standing above to those walking on Earth and, at the same time, bring renewing powers into the constitutions of those on the other side, who encounter the forces that he can transmit through the Earth.

The Archangel renews the life of the human mind when he is in the ascendant, working downwards. He quickens the life of the bodily constitution when he works from below into the region of the will. From both directions these spiritual beings, far wiser than we are, are continually renewing and renovating our forces, whether we inhabit the North or the South of the Earth. In the rhythm of the year the work of rehabilitation continues. Being human, we rise above what we are in ourselves because of their tireless help and support. In the world-conception of Rudolf Steiner, new insight is given into the human relationship to the spiritual beings of the Hierarchies above man. That we do not succumb to the strain of living on the Earth, that we are not ruined by the use we make of our faculties, is because of the patient tasks performed by the heavenly Hierarchies. Our human minds are easily dulled, but the inspiration of the Archangel presiding over each season wakens fresh thoughts and feelings. At the same time the human constitution would languish if it were not nourished from below by what an Archangel can perform in the process of reconstruction. In crude language, it might be said that the human being wears himself out in mind and body, but an Archangel comes to restore him. In daily existence a person realizes that he alternates between sensations of well-being and 'bad being'. He longs for well-being and is depressed when he feels the lack of it, but he remembers in our present time far too rarely what is restoring him through the work of the Archangels. We humans are not self-made, nor are we left alone. We continue to exist in a workshop of Archangels and with their assistance we think, feel and will.

The Archangel Gabriel calls down into human hearts the spiritual ideas from which we can distil the inspiration to understand and to find a sense of purpose. When he works from below, he can renew in us the mysterious power of nutrition. We digest and we are strengthened. To be worried with indigestion is a fairly common fate nowadays. To triumph over this worry is the achievement of an Archangel wishing to relieve man of an intolerable burden.

The Archangel Raphael inspires heart and mind with the great concept of restoration. Man is Heaven-born, but his being is sickened by the influences of materialism, which invade his soul when he lives on Earth. Raphael's power to heal inspires the heart with purposes for the future that give meaning to the earthly life of people. When this Archangel works below from the Earth, he strengthens the healing forces that are active in the capacity of the human body to breathe in and out. That which allows us to continue an earthly life resides in the will to go on breathing.

The Archangel Uriel awakens in the human heart the conscience which brings responsibility for the human portion of existence. Responsibility, which is borne by each one of us for what we do with our lives, is enlarged into the movement of conscience which we may feel towards human history itself. What do I make of my own life for good or ill? But, what do I contribute to the history of mankind through what I make of my own problems? When this Archangel works through the Earth, he cares for renewing the human ability to think. That which allows us to take part in the struggles of others, to understand and feel the outcome of history itself, all this part of the life of our mind depends upon what this Archangel, through his power of grace, can renew.

The Archangel Michael lets flow, from his own wealth of heart into our human will, the courage to turn thought into action. All that can be perceived and understood can make the human soul wiser, but one can only contribute to the welfare and progress of the world through that which one gives in action. The process by which one becomes wiser will not become that by which one can go into action without the development of courage. It is easy to feel fear and hard to overcome it. But the Archangel is at hand to help. When he is in the ascendent, he can inspire the will to courage in the human heart. When he works below through the Earth, he can condense the power of courage into the will to act. He can make a doubtful human soul into a hero. He is the guide and helper of those who are striving to develop the heroic in themselves.

When the mind grasps the picture of the double activity of the Archangels, the thought becomes real that the constitution of the Earth itself in the two halves of North and South is significant for human nature. The spiritual powers inspiring the human soul work from two directions, with two effects. The conscious mind can receive illumination from the character of four different Archangels. The human constitution can be rehabilitated through the working of four different kinds of will. Such influences are a gracious gift from those who work in the heavens and who are directed by the will of God. Human beings struggling in Earth existence receive blessings of which modern people are scarcely aware. Those who work in the universe receive little thanks, because the effects of their offerings have not sufficiently entered human consciousness. People today are dreamers and in need of waking up. The world conception which came through Rudolf Steiner stimulates the mind to awaken to the realization of the influences of these Archangels who work in the rhythm of the seasons. They maintain for human souls a worthwhile existence on Earth.

Within the wide and far-reaching perspective of world history put together by Rudolf Steiner, the opportunity is given to find a picture of Christ before His Incarnation on Earth. He worked powerfully in the heavens for the sake of man's history on Earth, before He descended into the earthly being of Jesus. He was working with the will of God from the Heights, for the good of mankind, that the earthly history should be directed with a true sense of purpose. Man was sent down to be born on Earth. Each human soul has been sent down to live on Earth with a heavenly purpose. Christ from the heavens has worked from the beginning of time to help humanity to know the purpose of Earth existence. When He walked on Earth as Jesus of Nazareth, He spoke of human souls as seeds planted in a new field. Just as seeds are planted with the intention of producing the harvest, so in the cosmic sense mankind has been planted on the Earth with the intention of producing a harvest needed in the heavens. When in one's human heart one asks oneself what one is here for, the answer is found in the parable of the sower and the seed.

Everyone who puts seeds into the soil is doing, in a very small way, what God has done on the larger scale by undertaking to plant the seed of mankind into the earthly soil, below and far from the heavens. But in the process by which the human being is created, a problem arose, as it would be called today. How could the earthly and heavenly natures of man so live together that he could function as spirit, soul and body in one being? Could man become physical and earthly while carrying a truly spiritual being within him? Must one pull against the other? Must one prevail over the other? How can the human soul handle the experiences of the physical body, without being overwhelmed? How could the spiritual talents be exercised in a body fraught with material instincts? Much of the behaviour of the early Christians contained the fear of this problem. But in the long cosmic process in which the human constitution was formed, the healing power of Christ was introduced. From His temple in the Sun, the emerging constitution of man received a healing touch. The body with all its functions and senses was formed into an instrument for the soul life. The soul became able to bring spiritual thoughts and feelings to consciousness. But dangers and disorders, known now as sickness, could still appear. Sickness was not to be confused with health, and thereby the need for healing could establish the true idea of human nature in which spirit, soul and body work together.

The threefold constitution of man, in spirit, soul and body, was created by the healing touch from the Sun of the Christ Being as man came down to Earth. Even while the human soul lives on Earth and is exposed to earthly experiences, the threefold balance is being created. But in life on Earth the soul is compelled to be aware of the contrast between creation and decadence. Just as in ordinary life a person must experience the process of wearing out, of falling apart, of being destroyed in the world around, so he will experience in his own being that which falls into decadence and that which allows for the new forces of creation. The human being must find his equilibrium between that which pulls up and that which drags down. He must face his cosmic situation here on Earth. That is to say, he stands on the knife edge between growth and decadence. Each one, without giving it much thought, is involved in preserving his inner balance as much as his outer. That which had been created from the Sun sphere as the human constitution was formed on Earth before the Being of Christ Himself descended and is strengthened and maintained in the activity of the four Archangels who move around the Earth. They continue the work of Christ, and are able to influence helpfully human souls from above, in their minds, and from below, through the Earth, by working on the constitution which upholds the spiritual life.

If they were not able to maintain their distinct activities in their dance round the Earth, their powers would only work from one direction, either from above or from below. Either the thoughts would be inspired, or the constitution would be upheld. But as servants of the work of Christ, they are inspired by the same pattern of manhood. Spirit, soul and body are enabled to work together, to live together, to be organized together, so that the bodily constitution may be the true vessel for the spiritual activity in the soul. The spirit finds its reflection in the constitution. Processes of consciousness can take place, but only if the forces of the constitution are renewed. The most delicate and wonderful processes happening on the Earth are those which proceed within the human being, allowing him to become spiritually active in a bodily form designed for the Earth. He has been so created and he has to be so maintained.

Archangels and Symbols

The four Archangels each have a different function, in accordance with their characters, in their service to man. They are each separately his benefactors. As they move rhythmically in their relationship to each other, as each contributes his part to the dance of the whole, they serve the work of Christ together in community. They continue the ministry of healing, which was first instituted from the temple of the Sun and is now directed towards the mission of the Christ enacted on Earth. They are the healers and inspirers of our human nature and so deserve the benediction of thanks from our side. Their place is in the heavens, they work divinely, and they should have more recognition than people of today, tending to be awkward about divine things, know properly how to offer. A new doctrine of the Hierarchies is needed. Rudolf Steiner's vision of world history, where human and divine beings can be seen in relation to each other, allows a doctrine to be formed again. Each individual has to find his own apprehension of what this means. New doctrines today have to be discovered and not asserted but, when found, new customs of celebrating and acknowledging the work of heavenly beings can be discovered.

In an old and a new sense, their symbols of character may be found again. Gabriel holds the lily, which tells in a picture of the pure forces in the universe, which can descend by Grace to those who struggle on the Earth. Raphael holds the staff with the two snakes moving up and down, which is the oldest symbol of healing. Uriel, who carries in himself the sense of history from the beginning to the end of time, stands in the Sun where the sunbeams proceed to shine in all directions. Michael holds the sword. He verifies the idea of William Blake in his poem 'Jerusalem', where the sword is called the instrument of building anew. To build with the sword is to cut away what is useless and wield the forces of new creation with a purpose for the future. Where such symbols are given an artistic expression, the four great Archangels are recognized and acknowledged. They are acknowledged likewise when their special activities are made known. Gabriel announces. He has long been accepted as the Angel of Annunciation. Raphael explains. He accepts the questioning of human minds. He represents the harmonies of the universe. He answers the need for cosmic knowledge in earthly hearts. Uriel puts the question. He rouses the power of insight and judgement in the hearts who acknowledge his questions. He calls on the human sense of responsibility. Man's soul has come to Earth with a task. He wakens to the question of Uriel. Michael beckons. He is the guardian against error and the influence of evil, but he promises a new and greater understanding of the Mystery of Christ. So much has long gone unapprehended. A larger range of thought is required. All narrow concepts require enlarging. Minds and hearts are challenged by this Archangel. He gives the courage to face thoughts of heroic dimensions.

These four Archangels can be associated with music of different kinds. Gabriel hears the trumpets. In the great pictures shown to John in the Book of Revelation, trumpets are the instruments of Angels and other great beings wishing to make known to human ears the wisdom of the universe. Raphael holds the lyre, or its larger counterpart, the harp. In very early times the belief is recorded that such music had harmonizing effects on the organs of the body. It is the music of healing. Uriel is connected with the organ which in modern times has its counterpart in the piano. One instrument can in this sense carry the whole of music, as it is understood today. Michael is related to stringed instruments, in which the sounding of the universe is reflected in the whole orchestra. Music of these different natures honours the different characters of these Archangels. Music is not for one, but for all, though differently expressed for each. In the Book of Revelation to St John, musical instruments are differentiated according to their place in the universe. One kind of music holds within it the whole, and that is singing. All the living beings of the universe are pictured gathered round the Being of God Himself, who is known as 'He who sits upon the Throne'. They are assembled together by singing and the whole assembly is formed into a choir. The heavens are described as full of song. When there appear among the heavenly throng human souls who, out of their struggles on Earth, are, as it were, qualified to meet the heavenly choir, they also sing. But it is said that they sing a new song, never heard before, around the Throne in Heaven. The community of human souls on Earth has learnt to sing, but what it sings represents what could only be learnt on the Earth, in the world below. It is a heavenly picture of the earthly task of mankind to evolve out of the experiences of this world the new song that can be heard in the heavens. The song of the heavens is enriched.

Certain animals have been associated with the character of these Archangels. Gabriel is represented by the sheep. Shepherds tending their sheep heard the song of Angels in the night of Christmas. The quiet modesty of the sheep is related to the gentleness of this Archangel, who announces. The picture of Christ on Earth in the Book of Revelation is the Lamb of God, as He appears descending to the Earth, holding His divine power secret, that mankind should meet in Him the bringer of loving-kindness. Raphael, the bringer of healing, is connected with the dog. In the old story of Tobias, who was led on his hard journey by the Archangel Raphael in human guise, the young man's dog goes faithfully with him to the end of the journey. The dog had the gift of giving faithful companionship, of being at hand when needed to heal the pains of life. Uriel is connected with the lion, with the greatness of heart that encompasses the whole of human history. The lion down the ages has given dignity wherever he appears. Michael is associated with the horse, the intelligent creature who gives the bravest service to the rider in times of fear and of courage. The oldest known celebration of Michaelmas was horse riding.

There are many games from the past which children today are happy to play. Certain of these old games can be associated with the workings of these Archangels. All forms of hide-and-seek, of finding what has been lost, of moving between dark and light, have the character connected with Gabriel. All that involves movement of a rhythmic kind, where the body with its weight is lifted up into rhythms, is related to the character of Raphael. Skipping and hopscotch are the kinds of game that children tend to look for at his season. The character of Uriel, with his feeling for the judgement in history, is reflected in games of choice, such as oranges and lemons. Each player has to choose between the two and will then at the conclusion take part in a tug-of-war. In the season of the Archangel Michael, there is a natural predilection for spinning tops and flying kites.

What can be a form of amusement is elevated into a dramatic experience when the kite flies into the sky and performs its own dance in the wind.

Archangels and Stories

In earlier times, when people could more readily think of the spiritual beings who are at work in our human existence, these four Archangels were related to human customs and practices. Many legends were built up around their characters. They can often be the means of finding pictures needed for the celebration of their works.

There is a good source of stories in what is known as 'The Apocryphal Gospels' about the Archangel Gabriel. The Oxford University Press has published a collection of these old manuscripts edited by M. R. James. It was once found necessary in the history of the Christian Church to establish an official list of the sacred writings that make up the Bible. Many traditions and much literature, which was not accepted into the Old and New Testaments, are still known and recognized under the term 'Apocrypha'. A recognizable difference between the text of the Bible and these other writings exists. They are composed in the character of legends rather than of history. They are stories of the imagination, describing inner realities without historical, outer facts. But they are splendid stories to illustrate the working of heavenly beings in earthly history.

Those legends that tell of the childhood of Jesus illustrate the influence of the Archangel Gabriel. The presence of the Child born in Bethlehem into life on Earth is represented as a rebirth of Paradise. In the old paintings the theme comes again and again of flowers blossoming in midwinter around the manger in Bethlehem. The ox and the ass in the stable are shown tending Him with loving care. The harshness of animal existence is quite removed. All the creatures of nature are represented in pictures and stories as fostering and loving the Child come from the heavens. On the flight into Egypt the fruit tree bends down its branches to offer the Child food from its fruit. The people, who still feel the power of nature in themselves, become gentle and kindly, greeting the heavenly harmony brought down to Earth by the Archangel Gabriel in the way pictured by the shepherds.

The best of all known stories relating to the Archangel Raphael is one from Jewish history. It concerns a family who were exiled from Nineveh after the tyrant had defeated the land of Judea. The father is a man of upright life, risking his own existence by caring for the sick and burying the dead among his fellow exiles. His young son, Tobias, is sent on a journey to another town by his father to fetch money owed to him from the past. A stranger is hired to accompany the young man. He is revealed later as the Archangel Raphael in person, who leads Tobias through many adventures. It turns out that what the young man acquires, through the trials that beset him, are certain secrets about healing. He is involved with a maiden from a further settlement of exiles from his own tribe, who is haunted by a demon. His father meanwhile has gone blind. The son is helped by the Archangel to bring home a medicine for that disease, which works successfully. The maiden is healed of madness and the father of blindness, because the young man is shown how to cure them by the Archangel. The young man is a fresh, innocent character but, because of the trials through which the Archangel leads him and because of his faithful courage, he becomes a healer. Without the intervention of Raphael, the story would be good, but ordinary. It is not really a human story; it is one about an Archangel to whom people with need were able to listen for help and advice. At the call of Raphael, good and innocent people are elevated to be representatives of the healing Archangel.

The Archangel who presides over good and evil, Uriel, can be represented by an ancient African legend. Strictly speaking, the story belongs to the secret doctrine of a certain tribe. It has become known through a book published in South Africa.* The writer had met a member of this tribe who had been educated to become a historian or story-teller of the fellow members of his people. He made public one of their treasures for better or for worse. It is to start with a very sad story. It concerns the fall of man, leading to evil ways and quarrels among people. These people illustrate the fallen nature of human souls who had already been driven out of Paradise. But, in a sense, they had not lost their innocence. Wickedness is said to have begun among the gods. The people are victims of the fall into evil and not its originators. They would have had, from a modern point of view, the right to blame the gods for involving them in the discovery of wickedness. They could not help themselves. Dreadful wars broke out among these deluded people and they were taught to invent weapons. One woman described in the story is really a goddess. She discovers the mystery of death. She loses in the fighting one beloved hero after another. Sorrow envelops her divine life. She feels the woe of wickedness. She recognizes the longing to demolish the enemies with her greater strength. She is tempted to long for vengeance, but something quite new is born in the deepest depths of sadness of the dilemma. Quite unexpectedly she is aware of a musical sound from the twanging of the bow. The other instruments also show her a new power of joy. She hears music.

Out of her new joy she discovers that each of the instruments of battle can be made to sound with notes of music. As they sound together, she

* Vusamazulu C. Mutwa, *Indaba My Children* (Blue Crane Books, Johannesburg 1964).

hears the first orchestra of the world. She is the goddess, it is said in the story, who became the giver of music. She discovers in her deep grief that weapons are not required to be laid aside, but transformed. The grief of destruction and death, the venom of vengeance, can be transformed and lifted, through the spiritual powers of the human heart, into music. It can comfort and give joy in the midst of misery. Discovered by the tragic goddess, it can become the grace of comfort and healing to mankind. The wisdom of the Archangel Uriel to reject evil grows into the power to change it into good. The magic of grief touches the dangerous weapons that they may sound in music.

Many are the legends about the Archangel Michael. Said to stand with one foot on the land and the other on the sea, he became the protector of everything that belongs to the places where the world ocean meets the firm mass of earth. He is also the one who is involved with encounters with the Devil. In some of these legends he gets the better of him by cleverness. The Devil is certainly very clever, but his view of the world is narrow and the Archangel is sustained by heavenly forces of wisdom and light. There is one legend of Russian origin which reveals as no other the majesty of his heavenly being. It is about the Crucifixion of Jesus Christ in Jerusalem. It tells not only of the perversely wicked people present on the hill of Golgotha, and of the sad and loving people who were the true friends of Jesus Christ, but it also describes the heavens above the Cross, filled with the ranks of the nine Hierarchies, gazing down in grief at what was happening on the Earth. In this story, one of the Archangels, Michael, descends down to the sphere where the Cross stands and refuses to ascend to the distant heavens. Just as one disciple is said to have leant on the breast of Jesus Christ at the Last Supper, so one of the Archangels remains near to Him on the Cross. The divine voice bids him to return to the heavens, but he will not withdraw. The measure of suffering possible on the Earth is made known to the Archangel. He experiences a passion of resistance, of anxiety to prevent, of the impulse to seek a just vengeance. But the voice from the Cross holds him back from action. He has entered the experience of suffering beyond that expected of an Archangel. He could withdraw into the heavens, but he cannot retreat. Only as the head on the Cross is bowed in death can the Archangel withdraw, casting, as he goes, his spear into the Temple and rending in two the veil within. Michael, of all the Archangels, is the one drawing nearest to the heart of Christ. He asks to understand the meaning of death and resurrection.

Such a picture is valuable for indicating that the Archangels are more than symbols. They are beings of character who change and develop as they exercise their divine office. The deed of Christ on Golgotha was not an event in the heavens, but on Earth. The heavenly beings who were so faithful to the service of Christ could follow His deeds on Earth and minister to His aims. Gabriel could bring the light of Paradise to shine upon Him in His ways on Earth. Raphael could make clear the strength to heal, working in His presence. Uriel could judge between good and evil, and advance to the understanding of how evil was to be redeemed. Michael could behold the death which became Resurrection. The Archangels grow and develop in character as they are at work actively in human existence on Earth. As they continue to give service to Christ, they are involved in changing and growing.

Archangels and Parables

Among the parables recorded in the Gospels are certain ones related to the characters of the four Archangels of the seasons. Parables are stories in pictures, composed and told by Jesus Christ Himself. They are expressions of His thinking, in the language of pictures. Certain of these stories belong especially to certain Archangels.

The character and task of the Archangel Gabriel is reflected in the story of the talents (St Matthew 25:14). It speaks of a man going on a journey, entrusting his servants with different portions of his wealth. The word 'talent' refers to coins used at the time of the Gospel stories. In the English language the word has now another meaning, which is most appropriate. Talents refers to gifts of the human personality of an inner kind. A talented person has capacities to deal with certain activities of human nature. The parable speaks of what is expected of the servants, to whom different numbers of talents have been allotted to use and increase them. Such pictures can be interpreted in many ways and one of them is the thought that it relates to what happens to a human soul when it is born into a body on Earth. Each one comes with a different set of capacities that he will be free to use or neglect in the years of his life on Earth. When the soul returns to the world from which he was born, he will see clearly what he has done, or not done, with the gifts with which he went out. The Archangel Gabriel presides over what descends from heaven to Earth. It is part of his character to lead human souls to the experience of setting out endowed with gifts and facing the question: what shall I do with them?

The Archangel Raphael is clearly related to the parable of the good Samaritan (St Luke 10:30). Birth is like setting forth on a journey, leaving behind the shelter of the heavens, going alone into the risks and uncertainties of life on Earth. There is the one who falls into dangers. Whether one regards him as having brought them on himself or not, he is the victim of robbers who make him helpless. The compassion of the other person, of the stranger who passes by, brings healing. The victim is restored to strength and enabled to stand on his own feet. How does the

Archangel Raphael use the forces of healing? The question is answered in the process of what the Samaritan does to help the victim.

The Archangel Uriel surveys the whole of human life and what he sees is reflected in the parable of the prodigal son (St Luke 15:11). The world of the heavens is reflected in the picture of the father's house, which the son leaves and to which he eventually returns. The world of the Earth into which we are born is represented in the picture of the far country. The helplessness of the son, far from home, is reflected in the problems of living in an unknown world. The birth gifts of the human soul are reflected in the wealth that the son brings with him. What he loses reflects his weakness of character when he faces the dilemmas of this unknown world. The prodigal son is in danger of becoming a wastrel. He is saved by the experience of coming to himself. Rousing up all his inner courage and strength, he returns by his own powers to the father's house. There he is given a hero's welcome. The Archangel Uriel, whose gaze sweeps from the creation of man to what may become his end in the heavenly world, sends a vision of what man can make of himself, out of the grief about the Fall, in the distant time to come. It is a great picture of the judgement that a person makes for himself about his own life, with the challenge to his own courage which accompanies it.

The Archangel Michael is related to the parable of the king's marriage feast (St Matthew:22). This story is about a marriage which the story-teller never describes. Its theme is the invitation which has gone out to many people to be present at this great event and to be guests at the feast. The story of the invitation begins very tragically. Invitations are sent by messenger to all the important people, who would, by ancient right, be invited. They show no interest, either in understanding or accepting the invitation. What is the king to do about the marriage feast of his son? The messengers return with gloomy tidings. Some do not return, because they have been slain in wrath by those invited. What does the king do? He sends his messengers out into the streets to bring in everyone, both bad and good. When the feast begins, there is a distinction made which the king takes very seriously. One of this odd lot of invited guests refuses to wear the wedding garment and expects to come as he is. When the king enquires how this comes to be, he turns out to be quite helpless. He cannot answer the question and he cannot speak. It is considered impossible that he should remain at the feast, and he is turned out. The story turns on the courage to perceive and accept opportunities. The Archangel Michael, the dispenser of courage, is active in opportunities for spiritual experiences and the need for development to meet them.

3

The Earth and her Seasons

To be aware of the changing seasons is to discover the Earth as a living being. For a dangerously long time, the Earth has been seen as a source of raw materials. Since industry was discovered and began to be acceptable all over the world, the ancient respect and regard for nature was suppressed. But it is beginning to return through those who discover the organic needs in the existence of the Earth, equally with its inorganic wealth. It was a long time ago in the Middle Ages when a certain picture was painted, which is still to be found in the British Museum.* It represents nature as a goddess in the form of a very bossy lady, who was instructing a highly nervous poet in what he should say about her. There are no nervous poets left today to whom it might occur that there is another kind of judgement about what they are saying. It is only just occurring again to modern people that there might be another judgement than theirs about what is being done in the world of nature.

The Earth is the Mother of Nature, but the Father is still in the universe. What happens in the course of the year is the interchange in their relationship. What we experience in nature is determined by the fact that we are their offspring. We, being human, who depend upon the interchange, should be able to offer, out of our understanding, sympathy and respect. The attitude that we have the right to take what we can get has already done enough damage. As an example taken from real life, it is possible to quote a conversation once held between several farmers. The subject was: how to treat a piece of pasture. All were involved in the organic methods of farming. In the conversation, some quoted methods of treatment for the pasture which had demonstrated an increase in growth and a better harvest. But one said that when it was a question of cultivation, one could go to the pasture and ask after its own well-being. When the pasture has been so treated that it has become more contented and happy in its own existence, the question of increase would be unnecessary.

* 'Dame Nature gives her orders to Genius' by Roman de la Rose.

The seasons are a continual reminder that the Earth is a living being, in whose existence cosmic powers and material ones meet. Of course in this age of technology modern people continually realize that the discomfort of changing seasons and variable weather can be overcome. The heating of buildings counteracts the cold of the winter. The means of transport are adjusted to deal with the changes of weather. When the seasonal atmosphere triumphs, it is considered to be disastrous. On the other hand, it is deemed commercially unfavourable if winter sports are not supported by the weather. Artificial snow has had to be invented. The forces of the summer are equally counteracted by such inventions as air-conditioning and swimming-pools. Nevertheless, sensitivity to the seasonal changes is part of our human nature. When it is allowed to operate, it calls to life our sympathy with the living being of the Earth.

The relationship of the Earth to the cosmos around it is a process of breathing. In the world of thought revealed by Rudolf Steiner, the Earth is to be seen in a continual interchange with the cosmic heavens, related to that which the single human being knows as breathing. In the whole year there is a long process of breathing in and another one of breathing out. From midsummer to midwinter, the living Earth takes a long breath inwards. Between midwinter and midsummer, another process of out-breathing continues. In the individual person breathing is a matter of air; in the whole Earth it is a matter of forces of growth and decay. While the Earth is taking in the forces of growth there is great activity in its inner being. Outwardly, there is little to show for this. But in the period when the Earth is breathing out, growth, flowering and fruiting characterize the changing season. When the outer activity begins to fade, the forces drawn into the Earth become more inward. That which is breathed in will later be breathed out. The process is echoed in the human constitution. During the periods of in-breathing, the human being has a natural inclination to the activity of understanding, thinking and conveying thoughts. In the season of out-breathing, the constitution shows a natural vigour in outer activity, in willing and performing deeds. Thinking and planning become more dependent on the inner character of each person.

The process is common to the whole Earth, but takes place at different times. When it is winter in the North, it is summer in the South. In the South, winter sets in while summer is appearing in the North. In both hemispheres the same processes are repeated, but the timing is different. A very important moment is reached in the course of the seasons when the out-breathing is completed and the in-breathing is just beginning. In the North this moment is reached in the Holy Nights; in the South the same process occurs at another time. In that moment, all has been finished which the Earth has received from the heavens. The leaves of the one season have fallen off the trees, the seeds have dropped into the Earth, the land is bare. Will the Earth be able to start breathing out again that which was received and prepared for a new season of blossoming and fruiting? The Earth holds her breath. There is a pause in the rhythm of the year. It passes away and once more the Earth can begin to breathe out again, bringing to growing life what the Earth soul carries within her. The process begins which will develop into spring and summer. That which is being breathed into the Earth begins to show itself in the growing and blossoming in nature.

That which adorns the Earth in spring and summer began when the Earth soul was drawn into the body and wakefulness of thought prevailed within the Earth. Cosmic inspiration from the heavens has woken within the Earth's soul in the process of breathing in. That which is displayed in the wonders of nature, when the soul breathes out, has been prepared within the thoughts of the Earth. But in the process of becoming physically real, the thoughts are no longer awake—they become dreams. The flowering meadow in the summer was once a field of thought in the inner life of the Earth. When the blossoms grow and develop, they become like pictures in dreams. There is a world of dreams in nature during the season of blossom and fruit, but they are Heaven-sent dreams sent down from the stars to be made visible for a while in shape and colour in the physical Earth. They are in the truest sense gifts from above. They come and they go, they blossom and fade, because such heavenly inspirations cannot abide in their physical form for long.

In the poetry inspired by nature, comments have often been made on the wonders of flowers, insects and animals, and how by their very nature they must fall quickly into decay. They adorn the Earth, they give to people heavenly joy, they disappear quickly and yet with the promise of return. In the pause between the in-breathing and out-breathing of the Earth, the heavenly promise of renewal is felt. What has gone away will come back. Or so it would be if nature were allowed to live her own life. But the certainties of nature are no longer secure. People can interfere. They have interfered. The wonders of nature can be destroyed by technically-minded people. The out-breathing and in-breathing of the Earth's soul is endangered. Why do human beings do themselves so much damage? Why do they have so little respect for Mother Earth?

The full interchange of the four seasons comes to clearest expression in the northern hemisphere. Wintertime can look as if it were autumn prolonged in the South. The old leaves on some trees are pushed off by the new ones under the thrust of spring. At the centre of the Earth on either side of the Equator, the interchange of the seasons becomes obscured. In the regions called the tropics, the impression is of a sustained summer. Likewise in the Arctic and Antarctic Circles at both ends of the Earth, the forces of winter hold a grip on nature during most of the year.

Nevertheless, it can be said that the four seasons are the expression of the changing relationship between the Earth—the cosmic place where human populations can grow and develop—and the heavens. A kind of conversation between the beings who dwell in the stars and those who dwell on the Earth is continued from season to season.

The movement of history now brings us to the time when people on the Earth will need to share in what is created in the universe in a new manner. No longer will they be able to receive benefits as a matter of course—they will have to do more to safeguard the rhythms. They will have to conduct their affairs out of a greater respect for the living quality of the Earth. They will have to respect her needs and help her to flourish. It is a matter of developing a consciousness more adjusted to the living processes. The live Earth is hostess to many creatures seeking forces of life. The Earth herself belongs much more closely to the heavens than is realized. Once upon a time the psalmist sang: 'The Earth is the Lord's and the fullness thereof.' He was speaking of a fact that will become a new discovery soon. Meanwhile, there is reality in speaking of the Earth as endangered.

The seasons speak the language of living and dying, of death and renewal. The stories of the Bible begin with a time when the Earth was alive in the universe. It was called 'Paradise'. As the story of the beginning continues in the Bible, a new element is introduced. The Serpent has appeared in Paradise. Under his influence the original couple, Adam and Eve, vital with the forces of the universe, encounter a new kind of consciousness and become acquainted with death. They can no longer continue to live in Paradise. According to what is said further, the Earth herself has to share their experience of death. The fall of man becomes the fall of the Earth. The Serpent has introduced them to the power of death. Paradise is withdrawn and from then onwards the Earth begins to pass through seasons of decay and renewal. Life and death are intermingled in nature and in the human constitution. The Earth lives in the contrast between decaying and living, and man can be aware of both forces at work within his own nature.

The Bible, which opens with the story of Paradise lost, ends with a vision of the future seen by St John, recorded in the Book of Revelation. He describes the Holy City, in which death will be no more. God and man will dwell together in this heavenly city. The heavenly light of the Sun will shine not upon it but from within it. The second part of the Bible is the story of how mankind, knowing death, will be transformed into a community of citizens who will be able to live in that city. Man will no longer know the intermingling of life and death. He will be transformed into a being of life and light. He who walks in the shadow of death today will be reborn into a new existence of heavenly life. How can this be? Between the beginning and the end of the story of the Bible, the greatest of all events is placed. It is the coming, from the heights of Heaven to the depths of Earth, of the Christ, who overcame death and achieved the Resurrection of life. The seasons in the course of the year follow the rhythm of decay and renewal in nature. But man is destined to take part in the drama of history in death overcome, in the life of resurrection begun. Nature breathes in the rhythm of living and dying, but man is on the way from birth to death towards resurrection. The human soul travels through the rhythms of the seasons towards the ultimate end, the Earth transformed into the Holy City.

The breathing of the Earth through the seasons brings harmony into the nature of the human soul. People who have the welfare of the Earth at heart, who can live with the rhythms of nature, can become wholesome in their outer and inner character. This was noticed once by a journalist, who reported in his newspaper on a visit to a very large flower show, one of the largest in the world. He remarked on the good will prevailing among the huge crowds. Such an experience was not to be found elsewhere and he ascribed it to the fact that those present were all nature lovers, concerned with the growing and care of plants, anxious for the health of the ground and for all that grows upon it. The healing forces radiating from their inner life brought harmony into their social behaviour so that they could become people of good will. To live actively with the seasons enlivens and informs social behaviour. Hearts are touched again by Paradise. Spring, summer, autumn, winter carry harmony into our Earth existence, allowing us to develop it in ourselves. But our human qualities need to be cultivated with intent.

4

The Life of the Elementals

It is the custom today to believe oneself to be living in a world of things. They can be counted, classified, reckoned up for their value in money, turned into possessions and, according to one's point of view, termed assets. Sometimes it would seem as if they represented what a person is worth. Such an attitude turns out to be shortsighted, for life embraces a reality to be reckoned with beyond the world of things. Fresh powers of imagination are needed to become aware of the processes of life in the Earth.

The present situation has come about through a long process in world history. Heaven and Earth have been falling apart ever since history took the turn which is described at the beginning of the Bible in the Book of Genesis. It is presented there in the picture of the Angel with the flaming sword guarding the gate between the world of life and the other, which has fallen into the grip of death. In the separated place of the Earth the power of death began to increase. The first recorded dying of a human being is, in terms of the Bible, the death of Abel, killed by his brother Cain. Life and death had fallen into human hands. As the Old Testament continues, more and more stress is put on how much involved with the powers of death mankind becomes from age to age. Most vividly of all is it described in the lamentations of Job.

Within this picture of history, the process of continuing separation between life on Earth and life in the heavens is developed. To be born has come to mean departing from the world of our origin in the heavens. It means entering the world of Earth to encounter the realities of death, to discover that man on Earth can bring death or life to his fellow man, according to his own will. The great creating beings of the universe have had to withdraw their presence from the world of the Earth that they have created. It is their memorial, but not their present abode. They continue to care for the future of mankind, but less directly than they once did. Nevertheless, the life of the Earth is rescued by an arrangement which did not exist at the beginning. The Earth has not become a thing; it is still a living being, because the higher beings who have withdrawn have sent in caretakers to represent them. The Earth has a physical nature which is cared for and watched over by what may be called the beings of the elements.

More imagination is required to think in terms of elements than of things. Nevertheless, they are known to us by experience. Someone standing under a cliff at the seaside watches how the moving waves beat against the solid rock. Such a person may even realize that the rocks are being broken up by the force of the sea. A similar experience is to be had by watching a waterfall. The force of the water running down over rocks and stones wears them away little by little. The solid matter of the ground resists the flowing energy of the water. One day the energy of life will win. Under other conditions the water will turn sluggish, its life force will be depleted. What will be left over will be a marsh. By observation one can see that solid ground has an entirely different character from running water. An experiment in observation can go further. Great breaths of air move over the spaces of the Earth. One can hear the wind, watch its movements and breathe it in and out. Through the air we hear sound and receive light. We know by direct experience the contrasts of heat and cold and varying temperatures in between. Each person is sustained by the inner warmth of his own blood. The mysterious relationship is felt between the warmth within and the warmth without. The origin of warmth, according to our observation, is fire. The process of burning destroys in the material sense and brings the life of warmth in another sense. In such simple observations the moving life of the elements becomes real and obvious.

The beings who enliven and let flow the processes can be noticed at work in the material world, or in the care of the higher beings who had to withdraw into the universe when the Earth fell into the grip of death. In the behaviour of the elements, people can become aware of what they owe to the caretakers from the heavens who have remained on Earth in spite of the great separation. They need to be acknowledged and respected, in order to carry on their vital activity. The influence of mechanisms has developed very fast in modern times. It is not unusual to hear the Earth described as a potential mechanism. The human constitution is in the same danger. The hospital is easily spoken of as a kind of garage where faulty mechanisms can be put right. The trouble with this way of thinking is that it repels the living beings of the elements. How can the elements continue their living activity? The elemental beings have guarded and taken care of our means of existence on the Earth. Things are changing. It is now time for human souls to begin to cherish and encourage the existence of these beings, who have been sent to maintain the living Earth.

One of the mysteries of our human existence in this world is that in the conditions of the fallen Earth, the caretaking ones lose direct access to the greater ones in the heavens from whom they are descended. Between themselves and the beings of their origin, human souls find their place. The inspiration to continue their cosmic task flows into the beings of the elements on Earth from the spirit-inspired souls of people. Through the spiritually-minded souls of people on Earth, the great beings of the Hierarchies can be aware of the caretakers whom they once sent down. People belong to both worlds. They travel between the two. They are sent down at birth and withdrawn again at death. They are coming and going on the spiritual ladder which the patriarch Jacob saw in his dream. Before birth and after death, human souls live with the great spiritual beings of the nine Hierarchies who do the will of God. Between birth and death, human souls share their earthly life with those who are the caretakers, who cherish vitality in the Earth. Through the spiritual talents of heart and mind, the citizens of the Earth call down from the heavens the powers that enable the elemental beings to continue with their task.

Earth, water, air and fire are not things but organs of spiritual vitality, enlivening the place of the Earth where life and death meet. To extend our human awareness from things to living realities has the effect of enlarging our responsibilities. The physical Earth is useful and gives to people what they need. But what does the Earth need to maintain her usefulness? What do the beings of the living Earth need that they may continue to represent the forces of heaven on Earth? Is a whole new sphere of human duty and responsibility being uncovered?

In the great struggle of mind continuing today to establish a new and more caring relationship to the world in which we live, a new knowledge is needed about the living beings who are at work. What are the needs of the plants and the animals, of the water, of the soil and the ground, which are so important to our human living? But beyond them all, of still further concern are the needs of the beings who direct earth, water, air and fire in the constitution of the world in which we live. Those who walk and ride over the Earth, those who dig and plant, those who reap and take, are concerned with this question, just as are those who receive and benefit. Does the experience that nature-lovers are often nicer and kinder people also suggest to us that to be friends with the beings of nature develops forces of value to the human heart?

In fact, the psychological functioning of a human being is involved with the activities of elemental beings on Earth. When someone dies, his soul is absorbed back into the cosmos from which it emerged when he was born. The largest transformations in the soul life are experienced both when the human soul comes down to Earth and when the soul goes through the gate of death. 'We go back to where we came from' is the simplest version of the facts of our existence. What does it mean? One kind of consciousness is needed to be an effective citizen on Earth. Another is required when, freed from the body, the soul is absorbed into the existence of the nine Hierarchies in the heavens. Making such a big change requires their helping action in the heavens and, as the soul comes down to Earth, also the helping forces of elemental beings, who actively support the developing consciousness on Earth from below. Human souls can do little to help themselves at either of these turning points of existence. It becomes clear that man's existence on Earth is an enterprise of the heavenly world when it is realized, even to a small degree, how much is done to form and support his consciousness. Why should I depend so much on the support of beings living and moving outside my consciousness and consequently so often overlooked? The time is coming when a more active relationship will be needed.

The enterprise of mankind takes place in conditions not to be found anywhere else in the universe. Its purpose is a new kind of freedom which cannot develop in the universe itself, which is spiritually alive throughout. It requires the condition that spiritual reality is withdrawn so that human souls can seek for themselves, learn by their mistakes and act on their own resolves. In the parable of the prodigal son this is called the far country and its condition is only indicated. But at the start of the story, it is said of the son who left home that in the midst of his desolation he came to himself. But in circumstances where the influence of death is always present, the conditions which can lead to freedom require special support from beneath the level of human consciousness. What a person can achieve by himself and for himself requires help from the elemental beings who handle the affairs of the physical world. Rudolf Steiner, who was an expert not only in discerning what happens below the level of human consciousness but also what the mind can encounter above the level of human, intelligent awareness, could point to certain facts not easily discovered. The use of intelligence in earthly life depends on the manner in which ideas can become accessible from above. But intelligent thought, having been aroused, can easily disappear. In ordinary experience we can readily forget our thoughts, but that we can retain them, or find them again, is due to the operation of certain elemental beings under the Earth. Spiritual beings from outside the Earth are the guardians of ideas. But what they can give is retained by forces beyond the human mind in the care of beings of the elements working from below. The beings from above send inspiration into the human minds on Earth, but from below comes the strength to retain them, to think them over, to work them out, to transform them into human wisdom. We people on Earth are working in the dark as we handle, arrange and turn into motives our thoughts. We are left with the error of believing that we have done it all ourselves and have everything under our own control.

How does it come about that we live in such ignorance? Rudolf Steiner, who was a courageous pioneer, penetrated the shadows of ignorance and described how very ugly, hard to bear and disquieting is the appearance of the beings who help us to hold our thoughts. The confidence in being human could very well be injured or destroyed by facing up to much that lives and moves in the subconscious mind at work beneath our intelligence. This cosmic condition at work within us is necessary at the present stage of evolution. Steiner compared it to what happens in the soil from which plants and trees grow and where animals are nourished. It happens easily enough in a generation of town-dwellers that people going into the country at certain seasons are revolted by the smell and sight of manure being spread over the fields. But the same people will admire at a later stage the flowers in the meadow and the corn in the field. Only if they are wise enough will they face the fact that manure is necessary for the beautiful growth admired at the later season.

That which is found outside in the life of nature is a parable for the inner workings of the human consciousness. To retain and let grow the inspirations of great ideas, the human mind must collaborate with the ugliest forms of elemental beings, who can help retain the ideas needed to inspire wisdom in thought, in deed and in art. Art and science, as they are known on Earth, grow on a manure provided by the particular elemental beings that supply the force to retain thought in daily life on Earth. It is the nature of thinking to produce thoughts that can move on, just as it is the nature of the apple tree to produce blossom that will fall and allow the growth of fruit. The seasons mark the changes in nature. The enthusiasm of the heart encourages the changes in thought that will bear fruit in deed. Thoughts that do not affect the will are hollow theories. Actions devoid of thought do not sustain spiritual progress. Every benefit in art, science and religion grows for the future out of the inspiration received from above and sustained by the life of those beings working in the depths of the Earth.

But there is something else to be reckoned with. In the shadow world below our earthly consciousness there is disturbance and conflict. Each type of being active there must work with those of his own type and against those whose capacities are different. There is no peace in the underworld. The beings alive in the elements are striving this way and that for their own progress. They are eager to become different from what they are now. There is some reality in those old fairy stories which describe beings of the elements wishing to become human souls. The region of mankind on Earth is above them. Those who want to get above will be willing or anxious to haunt the human race. These are the clever ones, to whom the behaviour of human beings on Earth seems incredibly stupid. The Earth could not have been formed without wisdom and a portion of it has sunk into the ground. Rudolf Steiner described such processes in modern times. In an earlier age, especially in the East, pictures were painted out of the old tradition of the harrowing of Hell. It was felt that Christ had the divine strength to move in this area on the way to Resurrection.

The mysterious history being made in this region, where cosmic purposes enter the world of shadows, is enacted among the vital activities of beings confined to the processes happening beneath the Earth. On the surface of the Earth, the human mind carries on a constant search for truth, beauty and goodness, whereas below the surface, it would be true to say that truth, beauty and goodness are the flowers that grow and blossom out of the manure existing where the beings of the elements live in vital, confusing conflict. How can the ideals for which human souls strive in history be expressed? What is truth, but the striving in the human mind to give thinking its proper value? What is beauty, but the searching of the human heart to create out of true longing? What is goodness, but the hope of turning creative faith into action? They can be expressed as principles, they can be felt as longings, they can be active in endeavours. And when is the human being worthy of being human, except when he is exerting his powers for such a purpose? And where is the manure uplifted and redeemed, except in the beauty of the blossom and the value of the fruit?

Contemplating the Elementals

Accepting the guidance of Rudolf Steiner in this matter, it is possible to put together a picture in words of how the plant grows out of the ground, bears its blossom and then its seed, with the help of the elemental beings. Accepting such a picture in thought can produce a living relationship to the work of these beings. It can also guide the mind to a truer perception of what plants are in the life of the Earth. The picture is put into words for the sake of awakening a stronger consciousness of what a plant truly is and becomes through the work of gnomes, undines, sylphs and salamanders.

It has to be accepted that the gnomes are root spirits, very active in the mineral element of the Earth. They are not visible to human senses nowadays, because these are not related, as they once were, to faculties of second sight. It is necessary to imagine in thought that which is outside the range of the senses. With their help we see the wonderful appearance of the plants that grow when the winter has passed.

In terms of consciousness the gnomes are filled with spirituality. They perceive and understand in one process. They grasp ideas coming to them from spiritual influences. They carry the ideas of the whole universe as they penetrate the Earth. Plants are to them as light is to human souls. The gnomes follow the light, because they are looking beyond the Earth itself.

They need light from above, because they hate the dark surrounding them among the roots of plants. They rejoice in the ideas that come down to them from the universe. In their contact with the souls of people, they despise human beings because they have to reflect upon ideas before they can understand them. They themselves understand as they see. Nevertheless, they are haunted by anxiety, as they feel threatened by the danger of turning into frogs and toads. With the energy with which they strive away from the Earth to avoid the danger, they push upwards the plants as they grow. By means of this description the human mind can share in the experience of being a gnome and can watch, in thought, what the plants receive through their efforts.

Such a picture is taken from *Man as Symphony of the Creative Word* (1923) by Rudolf Steiner. Although they hate the dark underground of the Earth, the gnomes are carrying the ideas of the heavens down into the dark. But the plants are growing upwards. They reach above to the watery element, where they find the water sprites, or undines. These do their work in the element of the moist air above the surface. They dwell in the water, or etheric, element. They also must experience an antipathy towards the element of earthly water around them. They are in danger of becoming fish. They are able to disperse the substances which are present in the air. In their antipathy, they push the plants further upwards from the ground. They surround the plants with their consciousness, but this is one of dreams. In active dreaming they surround the plants with the ideas which the gnomes have seized in thought. This is, in fact, a scientific process comprehended by the human mind in chemistry. They make chemical processes by bringing together and separating substances. In their dreams they perform chemistry. In a state of endless transformation in which they dream of the stars and the Sun, of warmth and of light, they carry the plant further in its formation.

But the plants grow up from the Earth into the air, in search of the light from above. The inhabitants of this region are called sylphs and they try to follow the moving currents of the air. They are drawn in sympathy to the sounds which are carried on the moving currents. In consciousness they appear to be asleep, but they follow eagerly the movements of birds. They are happy in the company of flying birds. They in their turn are inspired to sing by the company of the sylphs, who bring them their songs from the universe. Filled with sympathy for the growing plants, they bring to them the light from above. They can penetrate the substances produced by the undines from below with the ideal form which the plants should express on the Earth. They carry from the Sun the forms which have been thought out in the universe and, through the force of the light, allow them to appear among the growing plants. Instead of the antipathy experienced by the gnomes and the undines, they carry warmest sympathy through the moving air.

There are other spirits dwelling in the elements of warmth and light. They are the fire spirits, whose activity collects warmth and carries it into the blossoms of the plants. They work through the pollen, which provides them with little 'air ships' by which they give warmth to the seeds. In the plant it is collected by the stamens in the blossom and given over to the seeds and the ovary. If the mind avoids the materialistic picture of how fructification takes place in plants, then another one can arise. The fire spirits bring the warmth of the universe to meet the ideal form of the plant which has been carried down from above and therefore can percolate into the soil. The work of the gnomes and that of the fire spirits meet in the ground once the seed has fallen into the earth, when the gnomes receive from the sylphs and the undines the concept of the form thought out in the universe. There arises out of such thought-pictures an understanding of how the forces of Earth and Heaven work together in the creation of plants.

The fire spirits are naturally connected to the world of the insects, who fly about distributing warmth. They follow the fluttering of the butterflies and the flight of the bees as they flit from flower to flower. Whereas the sylphs experience their own activity through the birds, the fire spirits give brilliant, lively warmth to the insects they accompany. Each one receives a garment of light and warmth which is woven by the spirits of fire. The lively working of insects is much less obvious to the experience of the human senses. The highest forces of the universe are the most effective in nature but the most hidden on Earth. In the world above, however, the light created in space below shines most powerfully in the universe. The Earth below is not forgotten above, because this light is a continual reminder.

If this line of thought becomes real to the human heart, it can be summarized in the proverb 'The Earth is the Mother and the heavens the Father of all that is created among the plants below'. That is to say, through the working of the elementals Heaven and Earth are kept in a continual, creative working relationship to one another. Each human soul, who descended from the heavens to the Earth when he was born, is kept in touch with his heavenly home by the wonder of the plants and flowers, of the birds and the insects, to be met with on Earth. They are messengers reminding him of the truth expressed by the little boy who said: 'I haven't always lived here, you know, I used to live in Heaven.' The word pictures collected from the sayings of Rudolf Steiner will reveal their essential truth in contemplation, giving life to the impressions made upon the mind by the world outside.

Elemental Beings

SUN

Midsummer is here.
On the arch of the sky
I wend my high way.
The world's creatures rejoice
in the strength of my light.
They bring forth their beauty
at the touch of my warmth.

EARTH

Midsummer is here.
The bright Sun in his glory
calls forth his creatures
to appear in his sight.
World Father is he,
Earth Mother am I.
We cherish our children
through the seasons and years.

STONES

Out of midwinter
midsummer is come.
Remember midwinter
before you go on.

SUN

Turned away from the Earth
at midwinter was I,
deep in talk with the stars
as they wheel through the world.
Much from them I gathered
and stored deep in my heart;
their light shines in mine
their strength streams in my warmth.

EARTH

Turned away from the world
at midwinter was I,
in deep contemplation
and quiet I lived
while the stars from above

to my listening heart
whispered the secrets
of the summer to come.

STONES

What you at midwinter
heard said from the stars
we stones always hear
as we lie on the ground.

EARTH

What I thought midwinter
at midsummer is shown.
All my creatures come forth
to your Father the Sun.

SUN

You creatures of Earth
formed by thoughts from the stars
have grown up by the might
of my life-giving beams.
At midsummer now
one another we greet,
World Father, Earth Mother
and their children together.

STONES

We lie quiet on the ground.
The ground is quiet below.
From Heaven we have our shape.
To Heaven we turn our gaze.

CHORUS OF
GNOMES

We are the gnomes,
the friends of the stones,
going up and down
under the ground
where the metals flow
in veins through the rocks.
World secrets we hear,
world secrets we know;
how wise are the gnomes
who listen below.

PLANTS

We are the seeds
sending down roots,
pushing up shoots,
growing leaf on the stem,
crowning stalk with the flower.
Holding fast to the earth,
striving up towards the Sun,

we live and in living
give praise to the world.

CHORUS OF
UNDINES

We flow with the water,
we rise with the sap.
We form in the flowing,
we weave in the growing.
All that the water
as quickening gives
we let flow through the stem
and form in the leaves.

CHORUS OF
SYLPHS

We swirl in the air,
we weave with the light,
we waken the blossoms
to fragrant unfolding.
We give them their colours,
we teach them their shapes,
we surround them with joy
in the time of their flowering.

THE BIRD

All that streams
through the air
within me I bear
as I fly on my wings.
What I learn from the world
as I fly on the air
in my song I declare.

SYLPH TO BIRD

Creature of air
wait for me once.
Let us share secrets
embracing for joy.

(*They chase each other.*)

BUTTERFLY

Of sunshine
my wings are woven.
In sunlight
I flutter from leaf to flower.
To father Sun
I give myself gladly.

EARTH

Where are the great ones
who keep you in their care?
At the heart of the blossom

the seed must be quickened.

CHORUS OF
SALAMANDERS

From above we come
from the world fire itself
to bring life-giving warmth
to quicken on Earth
the holy secret
of the seed new formed,
of the little sheath
that safely enwraps
the germ of the future,
the promise of life to come.

SUN

The World Father himself
sends you his messengers
to bring to the Earth
the warmth from the world.

(*Salamanders go round and touch the plants.*)

SUN

Where are the creatures
endowed with movement
who hop, skip and jump?

CHORUS OF
ANIMALS

We are living and growing,
we are moving and breathing,
we are sensing and feeling
from end to end of the Earth.
We obey the order
by which we were created.
We follow the pattern
taught by our Mother Moon
to each of our kind.

EARTH

Now at midsummer
to you, World Father,
I bring all my creatures
to be enfolded
to be new quickened,
with your light from Heaven.

SUN

What do your creatures
give, Mother Earth,
as an offering to Heaven?

EARTH

Much have my creatures
received from Heaven

to give them life.
To you, World Father,
their gifts shall be made
that you may bring them
to the spheres of Heaven.

STONES

One treasure we offer
to the heavens who give it:
the forces of form
that have given us shape
shall stream upward again.

PLANTS

Fragrance we have to give
from each cup
open wide to the Sun.
Forces of life we have
that upward stream as we grow
and prolong their spiral way
up to the light-filled heights.

ANIMALS

All we have sensed and felt:
the pain and the pleasure of being,
hunger and eating of food,
exertion and quiet rest.
What limb and senses perceive
we bring to be offered here.

BIRD

My singing is my offering.

BUTTERFLY

The dust from my wings I will offer.

SUN

Your offerings shall stream
from the depths to the heights.
But one creature fails,
one voice from your choir.

CHILD

Midsummer is here.
The grass has grown high.
I run and I play
while the Sun sends light
to show me the way.

SUN

Midsummer is here.
All creatures are bringing
the gifts that they offer.
What will you give?

CHILD

I am only a child
who runs and plays.
I have nothing to give.

SUN

You live and you move
and you give without knowing.
What have you thought and done today?

CHILD

I ran away from my mother
when she called to stop me.
I pushed over my sister
when she wanted to follow me.
I threw stones at the ducks
when they swam away from me.

SUN

None of this can my sunbeams
bear up towards the light.
You have done black things
That drop down into darkness.

CHILD

I have picked some flowers
for our sick neighbour,
and half of the strawberries
I found on the hillside
I keep for my sister.
My mother will know
how sorry I am,
for when I come home
I shall give her a kiss.

SUN

My sunbeams will gather
all that belongs to the light
out of your heart
and carry it upwards.
What is good in human hearts
is the midsummer gift
Father Sun will take up
to the Angels of Heaven.

EARTH

Now at midsummer
to you, World Father,
our gifts we bring
that you carry to Heaven.
What will you give us again
in answer?
We receive our life

from the heights above.

STONES   Give us the strength of form
                  that our might may not cease.

SUN   The strength of form shall flow
                  to you from the heights.

PLANTS   Give us the colours of the light
                  and the joy of your warmth.

SUN   The light from the heights
                  shall give you colour.
                  The warmth from the heights
                  shall give you life.

ANIMALS   Give us the power of life
                  that flows on the moving air.

SUN   The flowing air shall bring
                  the power of life that moves
                  in your limbs and quickens
                  the sense for pleasure and pain.

SALAMANDERS   While the Sun sends down
                  his power to the Earth
                  we will weave in the warmth.

SYLPHS   While the Sun sends down
                  his power on the Earth
                  we will weave with the light.

UNDINES   While the Earth continues
                  to nourish her creatures
                  we will flow in the water.

GNOMES   While the Earth continues
                  to nourish her creatures
                  we will work in the ground.

CHILD   While the Sun shines down
                  and the Earth upholds
                  I will seek what is good.

SUN   Look up, dear child,
                  when the night comes on.
                  Bright stars you will see
                  that shoot through the sky
                  and fall down to the Earth.

Bright sparks from the stars
falling into your heart
will quicken your courage
to seek what is good
and do what is right.
From an Angel of God
the gift is sent down
into your heart from the falling stars.

EARTH

By your heavenly gifts,
dear Sun, we shall live,
and to you shall be given
our thanks and our love.
My creatures look up
to World Father, the Sun,
and say your thanks.

CREATURES
TOGETHER

Midsummer is here.
We look up to the heights
giving our thanks
and receiving again
God's blessing of light.
We live from the light.
We bring forth in the light
our strength and our beauty.
Dear Father Sun,
dear Mother Earth,
we give praise with you
to the light of the world.

(*Sing: 'All creatures of our God and King'.*)

5

Composing Festivals

At the present time, it is being discovered that festivals can still have a meaning even for modern life. The Reformation had its good purpose in history, but its influence destroyed the old customs of acknowledging festivals in the course of the Christian year. Some old ones are still revived, but we are long past the age when the holy-day was a holi-day. It becomes a task for us to re-create festivals in our lives which can bring back the experiences of holiness in earthly life. In olden times this came by way of nature but now has to be re-created by understanding. Celebrating festivals becomes a deliberate intention for which people make themselves responsible.

It is perfectly possible to compose ways of celebrating festivals in a variety of styles which can bring the opportunity for making new discoveries and making new developments from year to year. It is a pity to have one fixed form that becomes impervious to change. To avoid this, an attempt will be made to put together the materials that are available for each of the festivals and to leave the actual method of celebration to the imagination of different people under varying circumstances. In this way, there will be no right thing but many opportunities for discovery. The old way of holding festivals depended on the natural instincts that can still be observed in very young children. Nowadays, understanding of the spiritual reality within the festival should be the source of inspiration. The study of the Christian year can stimulate imaginative thoughts, valuable and useful.

The question is: with what means do we celebrate? An answer of some sort would be to say that we could call upon music, drama, gesture and movement, singing, Eurythmy, light, fire and games. One might even add special food, which expresses more than the experience of eating. Sensitivity to spiritual realities can direct the use of these ingredients. It will reveal the spiritual symbolism in earthly things. Take, for instance, the use of the hand. Holding, taking, giving are all uses of the hand, but they can become an expression of inner and holy experiences. To shake hands with another person is to make a movement which establishes a relationship of soul to soul, of person to person. Shaking hands has become the acknowledgment of the person to whom the hand is offered. He will accept the recognition of himself in the physical contact.

That supposes that the person who gives his hand is not, as often happens, merely expressing himself, either by exerting a hearty pressure or withdrawing into himself by the weakness of his handshake. The hand held out should be strong in regard for the other person. Each person who shakes hands is responsible for what is expressed in the gesture. He is reaching out to a fellow man.

Feet can also express spirituality. The footsteps of another person heard from afar speak of his character, of the impression he is making on the people around him and on the world around him. Hastening, pausing, turning, celebrate what the foot is doing in the world around. Out of these possibilities of foot and hand, the old folk-dances were composed. Nowadays, such dances can be repeated, or they can pass over into the dancing that belongs to the future, called Eurythmy. As this study is one which is looking towards new development, Eurythmy can be highly valued, but the old folk-dances can still prepare the way for it. Movements that go beyond the utilitarian become expressions of holiness. Contemplating the meaning of a festival can allow for the discovery of movements of greater meaning.

What follows is intended to point out how those wishing to celebrate festivals can arrive at their own imaginative way of doing it, just as much as they can follow customs. It is hoped that these examples will help develop many personal discoveries that will encourage others to do the same.

Advent

This festival requires a wreath representing the whole circle of the year. The material used should be selected according to the district in which it is being made; it is advisable to take what the surroundings can offer, instead of imitating the custom of the northern lands, where fir trees are common. Whatever kind of tree is found in the part of the Earth where the celebration is to be held will represent the daily life that makes up the whole year in that part of the world. The shape should be round, representing the whole. Four candles belong to such a wreath, because there are four seasons in the year. The candles should be lighted one by one for each of the four weeks of Advent. Those who like calendars may make one, to be opened each of the four weeks. Each should bring a picture that prepares the way for Christmas. The Advent wreath is for everyone who is present, but each may light his own personal candle at the wreath and use it for himself. An apple makes a suitable candlestick, because it points to the universal human story of the Garden in Paradise and the temptation which approached the first human pair, through the presence of the Serpent.

The wreath may be decorated with crystals that represent the geological nature of the Earth, with flowers that represent all that lives and grows, and with animals, carved or moulded, to represent the animal helpers of mankind. Still further, gifts that arise out of necessary daily life may be brought to the wreath as an offering.

Once upon a time, certain wood carvers made models of objects they required in their own daily life and offered them to the Advent wreath. Such treasures may have to be offered and accumulated from year to year. But they may also be given at Christmas to lonely and helpless people as a sign that they are not forgotten. The loneliness of people left on their own can be relieved by such holy gifts.

Christmas

Nowadays Christmas festivities are often brought forward too early. The correct time is from 24 December to 6 January, the period called the Holy Nights. To this period belongs the picture of the shepherds approaching the crib. The mystery of the night also has its place in this period. An old custom which can have a modern form is the one of hanging up stockings or bags to receive gifts that do not belong to the people round about, but which have the mysterious quality of appearing out of the dark. It is the small symbol of the great gift of the Father in the heavens to the people on the Earth of His Son, whose companions are the Angels, bringing Him from the light of Heaven to the darkness of the Earth.

The lighted candle is the finest symbol of Christmas. In the North it is lighted when the Sun sheds the weakest light on the world around. In the South the outer light of the Sun is very powerful, but the candle shines for the inner light within the heart, through which the light of the spirit prevails over the strength of the light outside. The lights on the Christmas tree are, both in North and South, the flowers of the spirit which shine on the tree of death, that the tree of the Fall will come to represent the tree of gifts.

Epiphany

At the festival of the Kings coming to greet the Child, the tree should be put away. In doing so, a candle may be lighted—the last one on the tree—

and each person present may give the candle to the one next to him. So the light of Christmas should be carried into the cycle of the year. The picture of Epiphany is of the Star, shining with the light of grace given to those who dwell on Earth. The Star should be greeted with song. The play about the journey of the Kings to find the Christ Child should take the place of the drama about the shepherds. Christmas is altogether a time for singing those songs called carols, but a distinction should be made between those that celebrate the story of the shepherds and those that celebrate the Star seen by the Wise Men. Epiphany can be concluded with a procession out into the world, led by the symbol of the Star and accompanied by a carol of hope that the Star will prevail in the world outside.

The Way from Christmas to Easter

Appropriate to this experience are stories of struggle to find what is lost, and games about the hunting of treasure. They may include the planting of seeds and bulbs. The seed has to be put into the Earth to die, until it can come up again as a new plant waiting to blossom. In the North, Easter and spring are naturally drawn together. In the South, Easter is drawn to the autumn. But there are many plants that grow from bulbs which are planted just then and they are quickened to life by the opposite season. They come into flower when the forces of winter inspire them.

Lent and Easter

Lent is the time of loss, and prepares for the revelation of Easter. Whether in the North or in the South, means can be found of representing the sense of loss—which was brought about in history by the Fall of Man into the grip of evil. Good is creative, but evil is destructive. And Easter brings a touch of the power to overcome destruction. Certain Celtic legends, which are memories of a pre-Christian time, stress this experience and are a good subject for drama.

Two gods discuss in the heavens their wish to go down to the Earth and see how people live there. But they have to remind each other that in the world below they will lose their divine appearance and seem to be beggars. Are they willing to meet as beggars? What about people? Are they overcome by a sense of guilt? Will they acknowledge the damage done to Mother Earth by human greed? Can they, or will they, put it right?

Easter begins with the ultimate, most fearful act of destruction. The Son of God, sent from the heavens to the Earth for the sake of mankind, is hung on the Cross. Weaker than the beggar, more badly used than the wicked man, helpless in front of His friends, the heavenly Son of God has to pass through the tragedy of Good Friday. Those who degraded Christ have degraded themselves. Can mankind ever be raised out of the greatest misery produced by itself? The transformation between Good Friday and Easter Sunday is the achievement of the Son of God. Those who should have stood around to help have failed. But the Risen One overcame, with His own deed, the power of death and the failure of His friends. The celebration of this event requires drama. For grown-up people, Easter may be celebrated as the greatest event in human history in a variety of dramas, such as the story of the Apostles, or heroic events from human history, also in great works of art, in poetry, in singing and in Eurythmy.

The lemniscate is the figure at the core of Easter. The urgent problem is how to deal with the powers of evil. What is their future? How can they be transformed?

Ascension

Easter is a secret of the Earth. It is made known to the Angels, the Archangels and the Company of Heaven through the ascension of the Risen One. He did not leave the Earth, for He united Himself with the future history of mankind, until, as He said Himself, the end of time. But the beings of the heavens are drawn into a new friendship with mankind through Christ Himself showing to them the meaning of the Resurrection. Every expression of praise that can be discovered belongs to this festival.

Whitsuntide

This festival celebrates the descent into the community of Christians of the Holy Spirit, that unites human hearts in understanding and in faith. A circle made in Eurythmy with the holding of hands can express this, as also can such a custom as reciting the Lord's Prayer in many languages.

The mystery of Easter requires much thought from grown-ups and will be beyond the thinking of young children. But there are customs that can prepare them for understanding in later life. Searching for eggs among flowers and bushes is a valuable one. There is a parable in nature which reflects the mystery of resurrection. The caterpillar weaves himself a shroud and within it is transformed into the butterfly, emerging from the chrysalis. Children can become acquainted with Easter, but they will be readier to understand it with parables such as this.

St John's Tide

The festival of John the Baptist is the counterpart to Christmas, whether it falls in the North at midsummer or in the South at midwinter. It celebrates the fire of the spirit within the human mind and heart. It can appear in a symbol as a fire lighted outside the house in the world of nature. The fire should be lighted deliberately as a picture of the fire of the human spirit that is lighted within at Whitsuntide. The fire can be greeted with dancing and singing. The climax can be reached when people jump over the fire to celebrate the strength of the inner spirit in overcoming the weaknesses in human behaviour. Unfortunate words and deeds, impulses of fear and anger, can be sacrificed in the flames for the sake of bringing to life in the soul the true picture of man.

Michaelmas

In the North, the festival of the harvest takes place in the season when darkness is increasing. In the South, the promise of increasing daylight comes with the growing of plants and seeds that will produce the harvest. But beyond the season, the message of Michaelmas relates to the growing courage of the human heart to withstand the powers of evil. What to do with the Dragon is the question to mankind at this festival. The Archangel Michael puts the Dragon under his feet. He does not destroy or kill it; he pushes it down. In this gesture, he calls upon mankind to transform what the Dragon puts into the world. The Archangel brings, in another gesture, the answer to the question. In the coming of Christ to the Earth, in His death and resurrection, the power to overcome and transform is given to the followers of Christ in the world of the Earth. The great future task of Christianity, the ideals for the future, are laid into human hearts and protected with courage. So the festival of Michaelmas stands at the end of the Christian year. Its festivities are in the area of drama and music with the theme of overcoming the powers of the Dragon by courage and transforming them by devotion to the good.

What to do with the Dragon

In Heaven a group of Angels.

ANGELS	What a bother what a bother, the stars are quaking, the heavens are shaking, our work is undone as soon as begun. Who brings the trouble, who makes the muddle?
ARCHANGEL	The Dragon brings trouble, he makes the muddle.
ANGELS	Stop him, stop him.
ARCHANGEL	Who will stop him, rampaging about with roar and with rout?
ANGELS	Great ones, lordly ones help us with speed. *(The Dragon comes by with demons making a noise.)*
DRAGON AND DEMONS	Rabadacabra, rabadacabra.
ANGELS	Ooh, he is getting bigger and bigger. *(Three Archangels in a group, Gabriel, Uriel, Raphael.)*
ARCHANGELS *(together)*	We heard you calling, we heard him roaring.
GABRIEL	My work is done through the power of the Moon bringing life to the Earth.
URIEL	My work is done when the thoughts of God are made known through the world.

RAPHAEL	My work is done when sickness is healed. The Dragon keeps out of my way.
ARCHANGELS (*together*)	We are working God's will each by dint of his skill. Being powerless to fight we are sharing your plight. Let Michael with the sword, the fighter of the Lord, contend with the foe who works us such woe.

(*The Dragon and demons come back.*)

DEMONS (*to Angels*)	It's such fun, jostling the stars and shaking the constellations. Come and join us.

(*The Angels run around stopping their ears.*)

AN ANGEL (*to demons*)	You are making mischief.
DEMONS	Hooray for mischief.
ANGELS	It must be fun to make mischief.
DEMON	Come with us, to be a demon, look here.

(*He puts a demon's hat on the Angel's head and drags him away.*)

ANGEL	Stop, let me go back.
DRAGON	Rabadacabra.

(*Michael appears with sword.*)

MICHAEL	The power of the Lord gives strength to my sword. The Dragon makes trouble getting Heaven in a muddle, the stars in disarray, the planets in dismay, the Angels losing heart, the world falling apart. This must stop.

(*He holds the sword over the Dragon who is frozen in position.*)

Sun's light enfold me,
Sun's warmth uphold me,
that courage quicken,
that courage ripen,
into strength for the deed
to be done in Heaven.

DRAGON

Few words to say,
fighting is my way.
On with the fray.

(He and the demons start to fight with Michael but they get mixed up with each other and fight themselves. Michael stands over them. Dragon and demons are frozen.)

MICHAEL

What shall be done with the Dragon?
Can we slay him?

OTHERS

Oh no.

MICHAEL

Can we keep him?

OTHERS

Oh no.

MICHAEL

Can we bind him?

OTHERS

Oh no.

MICHAEL

Can we throw him out?

OTHERS

Where shall he go?

MICHAEL

Who will confront him,
where shall he go?

OTHERS

Send him below

MICHAEL

Down he shall go,
down, down below.

OTHERS

Down, down below.

(He and the Angels throw the Dragon down.)

DEMONS

Oh woe, oh woe.

DRAGON

Down we go to work our woe,
down is as good as up for working woe.

(A group of people busy with jobs.)

BAKER	Knead the dough and bake the bread.
TAILOR	Cut the stuff and sew the seams.
CARPENTER	Saw the wood, hammer the nails.
GARDENER	Dig the ground and sow the seed.
HOUSEWIFE	Clean the house and lay the table.
SCHOOLTEACHER	Call the children to come to school.
NURSE	Put them to bed and give them pills.
	(*They are happy and sing at their work: 'All things bright and beautiful'. Then they begin to be sad and start quarrelling.*)
BAKER	The bread does not rise.
TAILOR	There is no one to help me.
CARPENTER	You are getting in my way.
GARDENER	I'm much too tired.
HOUSEWIFE	You all make such a mess.
SCHOOLTEACHER	You don't do what I tell you.
NURSE	It's all gone wrong.
	(*The Dragon and demons come by.*)
DRAGON	Rabadacabra . . .
DEMONS	Ranting and roaring, hustling and bustling, troubling and muddling, wherever we're found, confusing, contorting, deranging, dispersing, exploding, upsetting, you find us around.
PEOPLE	What's this, what's this, a dreadful dragon. We don't want him.
BAKER	Where do you come from? Go away.
TAILOR	We want to be left alone.
CARPENTER	We got on well without you.

GARDENER	Why should we put up with you?
HOUSEWIFE	You will make a mess of everything.
SCHOOLTEACHER	You are in the wrong place. Who sent you?
NURSE	Stop all that noise.
DRAGON	Nowhere to come from but there, nowhere to stay but here.
DEMONS	Nowhere to stay but here.
DRAGON	Down we go to work our woe. Down is as good as up for working woe.
PEOPLE	What shall we do with the Dragon? He has nowhere better to go. The Angels threw him over. Who will help us now?
DEMONS	Oh, woe, oh, woe.
	(The Archangel Michael appears.)
MICHAEL	Sun's light enfold me. Sun's warmth uphold me, that courage quicken, that courage ripen, into strength for the deed to be done on Earth.
PEOPLE	What shall we do with him?
MICHAEL	Will you slay him?
PEOPLE	We cannot.
MICHAEL	Will you stop him?
PEOPLE	We cannot.
MICHAEL	Will you throw him out?
PEOPLE	We cannot.
MICHAEL	Confront him, confront him.
PEOPLE	How?
	(Michael sings an old round with some new words, and the others join in.)

'Come follow, follow, follow, follow me.
Call the Dragon, call the Dragon
where he too may busy be.'

(*The people set to work. Michael takes the Dragon to
each person.*)

DRAGON
(*to the baker*)   Let me heat the oven.
(*to the tailor*)   Sew with the machine.
(*to the carpenter*)   Change to power tools.
(*to the gardener*)   Discover the tractor.
(*to the housewife*)   Let the machine do the work..
(*to the schoolteacher*)   Have you heard of visual aids?
(*to the nurse*)   The same drug will do for everything.

DEMONS   Ranting and roaring,
                                       hustling and bustling,
                                       troubling and muddling,
                                       we want to be there,
                                       confusing, contorting,
                                       deranging, dispersing,
                                       exploding, upsetting,
                                       we're eager to help.

PEOPLE (*to Michael*)   Can we trust them?

MICHAEL   Sun's light enfold you,
                                       Sun's warmth uphold you,
                                       that courage quicken,
                                       that courage ripen
                                       into strength for the deeds
                                       to be done by people
                                       in whom God's goodness
                                       lives in abundance.

DRAGON   Rabacadabra . . .

(*Song sung all together: 'Come follow', etc.*)

6

Cosmic Psychology

Celebrating festivals is part of the conversation between Earth and the heavens, which is the true meaning of religion. This conversation is very ancient. According to the Book of Genesis it began when Cain and Abel became aware of their existence in the world outside Paradise. Adam and Eve had known what it was to live in the presence of God in the Garden of Paradise. They knew how the world had changed after they were expelled by the Cherub with the flaming sword. Cain and Abel knew the world outside and were obliged to deal with it as best they could, but they carried in their being the knowledge of God to whom they turned for direction after their exile began. They discovered death when Cain killed his brother Abel in anger. Although they could not return to Paradise, they knew that a heavenly part of their nature continued within them while they were developing their earthly capacities. They were of the heavens, while obliged to develop their earthbound nature.

Much stress is put nowadays upon the earthbound nature of man and on the intelligence with which earthly conditions are encountered. But within the human soul the heavenly capacities continue. Even in adverse circumstances they can make themselves felt. The Hierarchies, weaving in the life and being of the heavens, undertake deeds which descend into human souls on Earth, who, true to their origins, receive certain capacities created within the Company of Heaven. Nowadays the knowledge of earthly things is considered to be more useful than that of heavenly things. People today are involved in a powerful outbreak of materialism, which is against their inner nature. Rudolf Steiner became the pioneer of a new knowledge about the spiritual nature of mankind, thereby uncovering the heavenly characteristics hidden within the earthly in every modern person. Uncovering the cosmic psychology is a process discovered in the celebration of the festivals. Something is hidden within the human soul which is the effect of that which Angels, Archangels and all the Company of Heaven perform among themselves. We recognize them on Earth in certain capacities for the spiritual life. Sometimes they lie unused, but always they are there, striving to express themselves.

According to Rudolf Steiner's book *The Inner Realities of Evolution*, the original impulse among the Company of Heaven was the admiration for what is higher. This impulse has been shared with the human soul on Earth. In the early stages of life, the little child is filled with admiration for what another, more developed person can do. The child who cannot walk yet feels a surge of admiration towards the older children who can run. The one who cannot yet jump with two feet off the ground admires the one who can skip. The baby who coos is entranced by the person who can sing. The little child grows and develops by the strength of the urge to attain what is beyond him as he encounters those more capable than himself. Growth and development arise from the admiration for what others can do and know beyond one's own range. What one admires is always a challenge.

When admiration descends into the will, it becomes the urge to offer what one has within oneself to what is above and beyond oneself. Thereby the process of creation begins. Faith begins to be creative. The original example given by Rudolf Steiner is that which takes place in the cosmos when the spirits with a capacity for will offer themselves with enthusiasm for what is beyond them to the higher beings of wisdom. Will from below and wisdom from above create in the universe. Here is the heavenly origin of what happens on Earth when a human heart heeds the urge from within to do and to produce and learns at the same time the skill required for any accomplishment. He has offered the will force within him to the wisdom he has learnt. One may learn from others to whom one turns in admiration. One may learn from experience. One may look for inspiration higher than one has yet found. The effort to achieve wisdom begins by admiring what is higher and greater than oneself and then, when the wisdom has descended into one's own heart, the longing arises from the will to take hold of it and create with it. So the Spirits of Will, offering their power to the greater wisdom of those above them, set about creating the world. This process is handed to the human soul on Earth in imitation of what is above and beyond him.

Psychological hindrances can arise, however, with any type of satisfaction with oneself or with what has been achieved. Creative dissatisfaction leads to further creation, whereas contentment brings the process to a stop. Too much dissatisfaction can cause a person to give up in despair. Too much satisfaction can cause a contentment in which nothing further can be done. The point of view which says 'I have done what I intended to do, so here I stop' brings about an end. The other which says 'There is no chance of succeeding in my aim, therefore I give up' prevents the beginning. People in Europe who lived for years under governments claiming to have created a perfect society were frustrated by a situation which allowed for no change, because there could be no improvement.

This was the fate of those who were obliged to accept communism as the ideal. All moral decisions which depend upon doing the right thing are equally frustrated. No step forward, no progress towards a still higher aim, is contained in what is merely right. Only admiration for higher ideals of the good can lead on to what is greater. Any action performed can be as good, for that moment, as the doer is capable of achieving. If admiration awakens within him, he beholds what has not yet been achieved. In the world of Earth the religious impulse to reach out to the heavens sets in motion the process of offering the will to that which is higher, greater and more truly divine.

The greatest example of this process took place among the Hierarchies in the heavens. The Thrones, who bear will in their nature, made an offering in admiration of the Cherubim, who carry the highest wisdom within them. The whole hierarchy of beings known as the Spirits of Time, called Archai, was born of this offering, and out of the smoke of their sacrifice warmth was created in the cosmos. At a later stage the warmth of happiness was evolved. In the human soul on Earth, this has been reflected in enthusiasm. In the heart that feels enthusiasm, the willingness to offer, to give what one has, to give what one is, flourishes powerfully, unless the enthusiasm wears itself out. When enthusiasm is united with creative faith, it does not exhaust itself, because the process of creating renews enthusiasm. There is always more to come. When enthusiasm fires acts of will, then further aims are born out of those that were there at the beginning. In the human world, each human heart sees its own vision, responds with its own power of enthusiasm and can share the vision with others. If this is not so and mass emotion holds sway, however well it all began, the danger of misdeeds invades the situation. It is a divine gift to the human heart on Earth to feel and promote enthusiasm. But the offering of will to wisdom is needed at the foundation if all is to be directed towards a new creation out of ideals.

The warmth of enthusiasm produces out of itself the longing to give. But gifts are useless if they are not received. Once the foregoing situation had been produced in the universe out of the heart of the Sun, further beings were born among the Hierarchies, now called Archangels. They undertook to receive what was given with enthusiasm and to reflect it back as light. In doing so, they created the cosmic reality in space. They also created in the human soul the gift of consciousness, so that wisdom can reflect itself in the human mind as knowledge. Each human heart is responsible for finding and caring for its own store of knowledge. Knowledge is light in the mind that can shine into the darkness of the will forces where lies the strength to make decisions and carry them out. We are able to hold fast to what we already know and transform it with what we come to know by our enthusiasm for greater wisdom. That which lives in our mind of the wisdom we have recognized in the past shines again in the wisdom we now seek. If the mind allows itself to forget too much, then treasures of wisdom are left scattered along the path of a lifetime. Responsibility for what one knows should live in the growing soul that is still gathering new wisdom.

In the history of creation in the cosmos, another element entered into the behaviour of the Hierarchies. The offering, brought in admiration by the Spirits of Will to the higher wisdom, was not all accepted. Refusal is built into the history of the universe side by side with acceptance. This fact is likewise built into the experience of the human soul on Earth. Two effects of the cosmic refusal are described in the history of creation. The acceptance of the offering was united with the stream of time which presents itself to the human mind when the evolving process becomes a real experience. The refusal was in one sense an act of adherence to Eternity. The step down into the process of time was resisted and the human soul, descending in earthy experience with thought and deed into the rhythm of time, was counterbalanced by the act of cosmic wisdom that saved the connection of the soul with Eternity. That is one aspect of the act of refusal. But into the stream of history was placed the substance of will that had been offered, separated from the one who offered, and set loose into the universe by the process of refusal. This has later allowed for will that can be used in opposition. The refusal through which Eternity can still be a reality for us human souls has likewise made real the will that opposes.

Within the experience of the human soul there appears the impulse of resignation. It prevails in all situations of disappointment, loss, damage to hopes and aims, and that which darkens the experiences of life. Resignation is not just acceptance. If it can be taken hold of creatively, it becomes an ability to transform, sow seeds for the future, and make the sad and negative experience of the present into that which is a promise of resurgence. The human soul experiences creative faith and disappointment side by side, but creative responsibility is at the heart of the act of resignation. Sometimes the process is called success and failure, response and refusal, a move forward and a setback. All these are terms in ordinary human life which have their cosmic counterpart in the acts of acceptance and refusal performed among the heavenly Hierarchies. Both suffering and creation in joy are to be taken hold of by creative faith, for they concern that which is intended to be evolved through the souls who pass through human lifetimes on Earth. They are, in fact, the substances out of which, in time, true freedom can be created in the individual human heart.

A further effect in the human soul of the history made in the cosmos was that the dissatisfaction left over in the beings whose offering had been refused produced dissatisfaction and restlessness. Out of this, movement became a reality in the history of the universe, and the desire for continual change and movement appeared in the human heart. Satisfaction is stationary, but the distress of disappointment and hope not realized can produce the desire to move from one experience to another, from one act of knowledge to another, from one effort to create to another. Divine dissatisfaction has affected the character and behaviour of many great artists, explorers, discoverers and inventors in the past and the present. Happiness can give strength, but dissatisfaction urges us to go on. In the human heart both emotions can powerfully motivate us. We can ask: could we do without either? Has the behaviour among the Hierarchies been directed by the ultimate wisdom of God and have we received from the heavens the diverse forces needed to pursue our own history?

For what, in the great tribulation of Earth, are we intended? The parables told by Christ in the Gospels often describe the Earth as a field where new seed is planted from which a harvest is to be gathered. It is implied, in all the parables, that the owner of the field is God, and the sower, who brings the new seed, is a picture of Christ. The seed is the crowd of human souls on the Earth. The harvest is produced and gathered by them, but it is destined for the divine owner. From our human point of view, many different answers can be found to the question: why are we here, for what were we born? According to the parables, the answer would be that we are here to produce something in the field of Earth that is not to be found in the fields of the heavens. If one looks into the history of the heavens, in the same manner as one has looked at the history of the human soul on Earth, the answer could be given that the Earth provides the opportunity for individual human souls to produce the freedom which is not yet present in the heavens. Each one of us has the opportunity to develop what is properly called creative freedom. The word is often used today for outer conditions of circumstances that offer people liberty of action, but it is clear that this is not freedom in the highest sense, in the sense in which it would be the harvest gathered on the field of Earth. Freedom begins within the human soul before it can be expressed in the world outside. Freedom is what man creates as God creates, so that he stands, independent of his fears, in the light that shines from the heavens.

The Twelve

The representatives of the signs move into a circle and each says his name in the following order: Pisces, the Fish; Aries, the Ram; Taurus, the Bull; Gemini, the Twins; Cancer, the Crab; Leo, the Lion; Virgo, the Virgin; Libra, the Scales; Scorpio, the Scorpion; Sagittarius, the Archer; Capricorn, the Goat; Aquarius, the Waterman. The movement in Eurythmy for each sign may also be done here.

MOTHER EARTH   Thoughts move within me,
live, move, are,
pondered through winter
in quiet with awe.
Who gave thoughts
for winter contemplation?
The planets singing moved,
the stars in chorus sang.

SUN   Lonely Earth!
Hear my loving call,
feel my tender warmth
at start of winter.

MOTHER EARTH   My heart opens wide
at the great Sun's call.

SUN   Moving through the year
my royal eye falls
on every planet's course,
on every constellation.
In spring I turn to you
to draw your thoughts to me.

MOTHER EARTH   My thoughts in living shape
are hidden in my heart.
Shoots spring, leaves spread,
buds open wide.
The stars give form
and you give life.

FLOWERS (*with Eurythmy*)   Hidden in thought
we are in this Mother Earth,
waiting for the spring
to call us forth.

SUN   I feel the gaze of eyes
that follow my course
as I move through the world.

MOTHER EARTH   All stones and mineral things
spread out in space
gaze at the stars above
in constant contemplation.

STONES (*with Eurythmy*)   We lie motionless here
until a force shall move us.
We exist without life,
while life flows around us.
We behold the deeds of the stars
and contemplate their light.

SUN (*to Mother Earth*)   I watch your living creatures
as they move, jump, breathe,
rejoicing in their strength
finding life in activity.

MOTHER EARTH   All my moving creatures
feel the urge of hunger,
the content of satisfaction,
the surges of pain and joy.

BEASTS (*with Eurythmy*)   Moving and jumping,
lying and sleeping,
hungering, pursuing,
resting contented.
Breath breathing,
limbs moving,
scents scenting,
we are living in space,
in surges of joy,
in urges of pain.

MOTHER EARTH   Where are my human children
to whom more is given than to others?

CHILDREN   We are here, Mother Earth.

Tell us what we are given.

MOTHER EARTH

God made man,
twelvefold He made him.
Twelve are the circle of stars,
the starry signs of the zodiac,
from the twelve directions of which
man is made.

(She leads them to each sign in turn and the representatives of the signs declare what they have given to the human body.)

PISCES

I have given you feet to walk on the Earth.

ARIES

I have given you a head to think your thoughts.

TAURUS

I have given you a throat to speak and sing.

GEMINI

I have given you arms to work and wield.

CANCER

I have given you a breast for living breath.

LEO

I have given you a heart for life itself.

VIRGO

I have given you a stomach for food and strength.

LIBRA

I have given you hips for balance true.

SCORPIO

I have given you organs of life.

SAGITTARIUS

I have given you thighs to stand and move.

CAPRICORN

I have given you knees to bend and kneel.

AQUARIUS

I have given you legs to move and run.

CHILDREN *(in answer)*

We give thanks to Him who built the body.
We give thanks to the stars who gave the members.

(Then the Sun leads them again to the circle of the stars.)

SUN

Man is a living soul.
Twelve times his mind is blessed
from the twelve signs in the stars.

(He leads them in a different order.)

ARIES	Have faith in your thinking.
LIBRA	Build upon facts.
CANCER	Handle the substance.
CAPRICORN	Live from the worlds of the spirit.
AQUARIUS	Know the spirit of the world.
LEO	Touch and experience.
PISCES	Experience the spiritual.
VIRGO	Observe and recollect.
SAGITTARIUS	Realize the unities.
GEMINI	Calculate realities.
SCORPIO	Grasp the power of forces.
TAURUS	Exercise reason.
CHILDREN	We give thanks to Him who quickens the soul. We give thanks to the stars for streams of thought.

(The Sun leads the children outside the circle The representative of Scorpio leaves his place and goes round the circle on the outside. He beckons to Death, who comes from the distance. He goes round the signs, weaving in and out of them. Then he goes to the children and takes them round the circle, beginning at Pisces.)

DEATH (*at Pisces*)	God gave your feet and your living soul. I have hardened brain and bones.
(*at Aries*)	God gave your head and your living soul. I have hardened brain and bones.
(*at Taurus*)	God gave your throat and your living soul. I have hardened brain and bones.
(*at Gemini*)	God gave your arms and your living soul. I have hardened brain and bones.
(*at Cancer*)	God gave your breast and your living soul. I have hardened brain and bones.

(at Leo)	God gave your heart and your living soul. I have hardened brain and bones.
(at Virgo)	God gave your stomach and your living soul. I have hardened brain and bones.
(at Libra)	God gave your hips and your living soul. I have hardened brain and bones.
(at Scorpio)	God gave organs of life and your living soul. I have hardened brain and bones.
(at Sagittarius)	God gave your thighs and your living soul. I have hardened brain and bones.
(at Capricorn)	God gave your knees and your living soul. I have hardened brain and bones.
(at Aquarius)	God gave your legs and your living soul. I have hardened brain and bones.

(Mother Earth gathers the children around her.)

MOTHER EARTH

What shall become of my children
held in the grip of death?

SUN

God has sent His Son,
the spirit of the Sun,
to rescue the souls of men
from the power of death.
For all mankind's sake
twelve men were called
to the circle of His apostles,
twelve on Earth
for the twelve in the heavens.

(The Sun leads the children round the circle and they say the names of the Apostles, at each sign, one name: Pisces, Simon; Cancer, Judas; Scorpio, Thomas; Aries, Bartholemew; Leo, Peter; Sagittarius, Philip; Taurus, James the Less; Virgo, John; Capricorn, Matthew; Gemini, Andrew; Libra, James; Aquarius, Thaddeus. Then the Sun and Mother Earth stand in the centre of the circle with the children behind them. Death comes towards them with a gesture of menace.)

DEATH

My power shall grow strong
to destroy the light

	and threaten you all.
SUN	My power is light to bring life out of death. Death shall serve life.
DEATH	The power of matter is mine.
SUN	The power of spirit is mine.
	(*Death crosses to Mother Earth and the children.*)
DEATH	I bind them to matter and they shall be mine.
SUN	In the name of Him who came from the Sun to conquer the darkness of death, I restrain you.
	(*With a powerful gesture he prevents the resistance of Death and leads him outside the circle.*)
DEATH	You will never be rid of me.
	(*The Sun puts a chain round him.*)
SUN	Your force is restrained that you may work only to serve the good.
	(*The Sun puts Death in chains behind him.*)
SUN	The spirit of the Sun henceforth shall shine on the Earth, and the living souls of men shall shine with the spirit's light.
	(*The Sun leads the children round the signs, and they all say together the words appropriate to each sign.*)
CHILDREN (*at Pisces*)	I will shine in greatness of heart.
(*at Aries*)	I will shine in devotion.
(*at Taurus*)	I will shine in humility.
(*at Gemini*)	I will shine in endurance.
(*at Cancer*)	I will shine in selflessness.
(*at Leo*)	I will shine in compassion.

(*at Virgo*)	I will shine in courtesy.
(*at Libra*)	I will shine in contentment.
(*at Scorpio*)	I will shine in patience.
(*at Sagittarius*)	I will shine in discretion.
(*at Capricorn*)	I will shine in courage.
(*at Aquarius*)	I will shine in silence.

(*Geometrical forms in Eurythmy are now made by the twelve signs.*)

MOTHER EARTH

God made man
in the image of Himself
and gave him the strength of stones,
the life of the growing things,
the power to move and to feel.
He set his head towards Heaven
and his feet on the steady Earth.
Man shall give thanks to the Sun
and to Mother Earth below.
Their creatures shall follow him
and he shall give them love.

(*The Sun stands in front of the circle.*)

SUN

God made man
in spirit, soul and body.
Death entered in
to destroy body and soul.
The Son came to Earth
to bind the power of Death.
The spirit shall shine in man
as the light of the spirit shines
in the stars, who gave him life.

(*Concluding procession. Music.*)

7

Christ and the History of Man

Why does one say that no human being, however advanced, however great a prophet, could rescue mankind from the overwhelming dilemma which came about through the Fall of Man? How could so great a power of evil beset the inhabitants of the Earth that they were brought to the situation which is presented with such realism in the Book of Job? The people of the ancient world powerfully experienced the failure of mankind, compared with the wonder of the divine creation. A modern person, supposing he had taken part in the dialogue between Job and God, would probably have said: 'Am I, as a man, not one of your wonderful works?' In the world of nature, Job could admire the wonders of God. But in the world of human beings he could only see failure, compared with the original design. Had God abandoned man with the same hopelessness that both Job and his comforters regarded themselves? 'How then can man be righteous before God. How can he who is born of a woman be clean? . . . How much less man, who is a maggot, and the son of man, who is a worm!' (Job: 25).

Throughout the Old Testament the lamentations continue. The Psalms celebrate the goodness of God. Unworthy, unfortunate man will be rescued with divine mercy, not because he deserves it but because he is such a failure. The prophets speak more vigorously about the dilemma into which mankind brings itself through the wrong in human nature. They foresee help for man's unhappy situation, but in the uncertain and distant future. Nevertheless, they realize the dilemma that help can only be foreseen from God. Man has become a failure in the eyes of God and only by divine help can he be rescued. The Fall of Man and all that belongs to it is spoken of as a matter to be resolved only between Heaven and Earth, between God and man. Man is involved in something too big for him, way beyond his understanding and moral strength. Much as a man may deplore his own failure to live in the pattern appointed for him, he can neither help himself out of his difficulty nor find any great leader in history who can solve his problem.

The Fall of Man appears in the Bible to be a matter between God and man and Heaven and Earth, not to be solved in human history by human effort. In other religions outside the Bible, the same problem is seen, but in a different manner. What can a leader of the greatness of the Buddha undertake? He can achieve in himself so heavenly a transformation that he can leave the fallen world behind and ascend again to the world of Paradise from which man has fallen. He can retreat to the state before the Fall of Man, to the state which he had lost. He can show the way to other human souls, who will then know how to follow in his footsteps. All the good that those who follow this way can develop in themselves will allow them to qualify for the return to Paradise. They will follow their leader away from the fallen world into the original state from which they had fallen. The dilemma is still the same, but its solution is found in abandoning the fallen world altogether. Who can lead mankind from the fallen world into the unfallen, from temptation into innocence? Once again, the problem lies between God and man.

In the New Testament, a vital change is recorded. God has become man, that man may become God. The One is sent from the heavens to the Earth who can take upon Himself the troubled human history. The divine world has answered the human problem by sending from the heights the divine Son to take the human struggle on Himself. Man shall not return unchanged, but God shall descend to bring him help. A human being, bright with goodness, was found to offer his human nature as the earthly dwelling place of the Son of God. By means of the ritual act performed by John the Baptist through the rite of baptism in water, the body of Jesus became the human dwelling for the spirit of Christ. The Gospels record what Christ could undertake in earthly history through living in the body of Jesus. In the divine world among the gods, it had been recognized that the fall of Man was, in fact, a problem not to be solved by Man himself. It could be accepted as a concern which God and man had to face together.

Who, in fact, had let the power of evil loose in the world of the Earth, the world within which divine powers had planted the seed of mankind? That man was not yet conscious enough, nor strong enough, to deal with the influences of the Devil is related in the Book of Genesis. Adam and Eve, in their innocence, encountered the Serpent appearing among the branches of the Tree of Knowledge. He easily persuaded them to eat the forbidden fruit. They knew that it was forbidden, but they had not yet taken hold of the strength to say no. Living a life in harmony with their surroundings, they had not learnt rejection. God had allowed the Serpent to appear in the Garden of Eden. Man and God had between them produced the dilemma with which the Serpent had been allowed to confound them. Who is really responsible in this story? In a sense one can reply: man—that is, Adam and Eve—for the action, and God for the situation. Henceforth God and man will share together the need to confront the power of evil, to let it work for the development of history, but will take care to avoid the danger of perdition. God and man act together in confronting the power of the Devil. That which was aimed at dividing them is uniting them through the danger in which they have been placed. God has created the situation through unloosing the Devil's power. Do we need evil in our lives? It would seem that the powers in the heavens favour the obligation to struggle, which the Devil constantly presents. Is the famous saying that the best thing God ever did for man was to throw him out of Paradise supported by experience? If so, the return to Paradise, so often the theme in the old religions, must be judged a mistake.

It could be a matter for speculation how God and man would have been related to each other without the presence of the Devil. As it is, they have become partners in sharing the world with the Devil, while cherishing their own aims together. The enterprise of man on Earth is shared with God, because it cannot proceed in any other way. God is committed to salvation because the Devil is present. What will be the outcome? God, man and the Devil is the partnership that arose when man was driven out of Paradise. The Devil began to have his own way and God had to take part in man's life in a fallen world, because He had initiated the enterprise. From the time when man left Paradise, when the Earth began to fall away from the heavens, when the power of death had to be recognized, the history of the Earth and man's part in it became an undertaking in which God must always be present. If man is tempted to believe that he is making the history of the Earth on his own, he is overlooking the realities of his cosmic situation.

The divine answer to the great problem of history has been to send from the heavens to the Earth the Son of God to take the dilemma on Himself. The great human leaders of history in the past could aim at leading mankind back to Paradise, but this is not the solution living in the heart of God and His Son. Christ came to create another future for mankind. Since the Earth had become isolated from the heavens through the expulsion of man from Paradise, it had become a dark planet. It had fallen out of the community of the heavens and become more and more influenced by the power of death. So estranged is this world that human souls cannot easily bear an Earth existence for very long. They must seek relief in sleep every night. After a number of years they must return to the world of their origin through the gate of death. Was the poet Novalis right when he said, 'Now comes death and makes us healthy again'? Nevertheless, the fallen Earth is the place where Christ and man endeavour in companionship to create the new future which can be made only in the perplexing world of the Earth. Christ, the Son of God, has descended to the fallen planet to create salvation here. It is possible, as the Buddha believed, to seek salvation by withdrawing. But the salvation of the future is to be created in the fallen world. For this Christ came. This is a matter for the heavens, which human souls on the Earth could not achieve by themselves. A God had to come in whom the spirit's power to create lived and worked, even as He entered the alienated world of the Earth.

The Gospels are the record of how the Son of God lived in a human body on Earth and how He became the creator of man's future. As they tell how the Son of God lived as a man, certain misunderstandings are possible. It has become a danger that such emphasis is put on the human behaviour of Jesus that the distinction between the man, Jesus, and the Son of God, Christ, becomes uncertain. The vision of Jesus Christ as the Son of God on Earth has become confused with the concept of Jesus being the perfect pattern of an earthly person. That Christ is the cosmic spirit dwelling in a human body on Earth, so that He may bring the presence of God into this alienated world, becomes obscure to the point that it is easy to believe that a perfect human being is enough for the salvation of all. Such a thought denies the terrible importance of the Fall of Man as it was experienced in the past by the great characters described in the Old Testament. Salvation is created by the Son of God in the fallen world of Earth through and with the fallen human souls, who have to find again their divine and spiritual being. The descent of Christ, the Son of God from the heavens, created the future in this place of alienation. Not a man but a God become man is the answer to the problem of the fallen condition. Man and God must labour together at the enterprise.

Jesus Christ was not as afraid of the fallen nature of man as were the people around him. The publicans and sinners roused His compassion more than other people. He could go without fear into their company. But at the Temptation, when He stood face to face with the Devil, He was equally without fear. Therefore, He was able to heal. He encountered suffering so powerfully that His touch brought healing. His compassion could work even in the domain of the flesh. He felt the power of death to the point of hanging on the Cross and dying. He faced the ultimate power of matter, which has produced death. He accepted the negation of the living spirit, but He won command of death, planting the seed of life where death had been. He commanded the great metamorphosis, which is called the Resurrection. He created the new salvation by overcoming. He described it Himself by saying: 'I have the keys of death and Hell' (Revelation: 1). The salvation that has been planted into the fallen Earth is the new creation, brought about by the enterprise in which God and man have joined together.

The Fall of Man is redeemed in the achievement of the Resurrection, which creates the new future of salvation here on the Earth. But the enterprise is still unfinished. Man has to work further with God in Christ to transform this world into a place where God and man will dwell together. In Imaginative thinking, which allows for cosmic realities to be represented in human minds, the true nature of the enterprise can be grasped. Christ and His Resurrection has made the Earth a holy place, where the divine enterprise can be realized in the time to come. This is the place of salvation. The whole human world has become its temple. Mankind is a community sharing in the process and thereby taking part in a common process of evolving.

The Fall of Man, so long held to be a curse, has been transformed by Christ, appearing from the heavens, into an opportunity. In the society of today our fallen nature tends to be greeted cheerfully. So many ways of enjoying oneself depend on calling up our less-than-human instincts, thus placing a continual burden of materialism on our thinking and feeling and inducing a continual boredom to which we become more and more prone. But to be afraid of human nature is no solution. The opportunity exists, in discovering the forces of transformation within, to uncover the truly spiritual part of our being. By developing on Earth the heavenly qualities in the soul, the curse is turned into an opportunity for growth. The fruits of a spiritual life, grown in the conditions of this fallen world, will produce seeds that can be offered to the heavens. Companionship between the two worlds introduces the opportunity for the new salvation produced here to be known in the world of the heavens. Overcoming the fear of the curse will bring the hope of creating a new kind of Heaven here below.

The Offering

CHORUS OF ANGELS
(OR A SINGLE ONE)
WITH FULL BASKET(S)

Baskets filled up
brims at their fullest,
scents overflowing,
tastes at their truest,
blossoms full blown,
fruits at their ripest,
brought as the offering,
the token of harvest.

Where ripened the fruit?
Where blossomed the field?
And where was the garden
that such increase would yield?

My heart was the garden,
my lifetime the ground,
where the blossom of goodness,
turned to fruit, will be found.

CHORUS OF ANGELS
(OR A SINGLE ONE)
WITH EMPTY
BASKET(S)

Our baskets are empty,
our blossoms were frosted,
the buds shrank unopened,
the fruit was all wasted.
There is nothing to offer,
no token of harvest,
no savour of goodness
to bring to the Highest.
The heart's garden is sunless,
its produce is blighted,
with evil intentions,
with wishes affrighted.
No angels can offer
what is blighted by evil,
rejected as dregs,
it is good for the Devil.

ANGELS (OR ANGEL) WITH HALF-FILLED BASKET(S)	Our baskets show sadly, our provision is least, what can be offered does not look of the best. How shamed are we Angels, but good actions shed light and goodness is cherished though the showing be slight. What shall be done with these remnants of good? How sadly we Angels bring all that we could.
ARCHANGEL	What shall I offer at the throne of God? What shall I declare to the Lordly Ones? The star-dwellers look earthward, they gaze down at the star-born below, asking: we gave them of our substance of life, we gave it graciously, but what do they give? What ascends from Earth to Heaven, what is the answer to Heaven from Earth?

(*He looks into the baskets.*)

ANGELS WITH FULL BASKETS	Receive our offerings.
ANGELS WITH EMPTY BASKETS	There is nothing, nothing here.
ANGELS WITH HALF-FULL BASKETS	Only the human people can do good. Angels must take what they can get.

(*The Archangel gathers the baskets and goes away. Two good-for-nothings come by.*)

FIRST GOOD-FOR-NOTHING	What are we here for?
SECOND GOOD-FOR-NOTHING	I often wonder what to do with myself.
FIRST GOOD-FOR-NOTHING	We are not like animals; they always know what to do with themselves.

SECOND GOOD-FOR-NOTHING	We exist, but what is it all about?

(The Angels with empty baskets begin to throw them away.)

ANGELS

No one brings goodness
to fill full our baskets.
No deeds of great meaning
are done to ease suffering.
We give up, we opt out,
we carry the baskets
but do nothing to fill them.
The good deeds of people,
the kindness of hearts
inspiring their prayers,
are the offerings we need.
There is nothing to bring.

(Two devils appear.)

LIGHT DEVIL

Listen to me.
You can be my servants,
bustling and busy, never sad.

DARK DEVIL

Listen to me.
You can be my servants,
obeying my orders,
never glad.

(The Angels with the empty baskets put on the clothing of demons.)

ANGELS *(chanting)*

Dreadful demons, soul-destroying,
trouble-makers, peace-disturbers,
good admiring, evil doing,
inclined to Angels, doomed to demons,
here we come to work our woe.

(They disappear.)

(A man called Dolorous comes into his room in great distress.)

DOLOROUS

At last I came away alone.
They had set on me from all sides.
No one heeded what I had to say,
or took account of my principles.

There was no accusation.
How could there be?
My responsibilities were carried out
without fail,
but I am out all the same,
discarded, rejected,
of no standing.
I am entirely alone now
since she went off,
complaining so often
of the narrow life here,
of the restrictions,
of my constant attention to my job.
It is loss all round and loneliness.

DARK DEVIL   Accept me as the Prince of this World.
                      Take the power of Mammon at its value,
                      for them and for me.

LIGHT DEVIL   Despise them, the mean spirited ones;
                      ignore them, rise above their opposition.

DOLOROUS   I thought to be alone.
                      Who are you?

DARK AND LIGHT   We are your life mates,
DEVILS (*together*)   at hand to put a word in at all times.

LIGHT DEVIL   You would do well to listen.
                      I can lift your head high
                      above the misery they provoke
                      with their sordid judgements.
                      Listen to me.

DARK DEVIL   You would do well to listen.
                      My advice is to your advantage.
                      You have tried to believe
                      that the power of money
                      is not everything,
                      but it really is.

LIGHT DEVIL   Do not stay here so sadly.
                      Escape with me.

DARK DEVIL   There is no escape.
                      You are back where you started.

DOLOROUS	I will not listen. You do not help, you haunt. Oh, who will help me?
DARK DEVIL	You have not lost me. Come my way.
LIGHT DEVIL	You will not lose me. Come with me.

(A stranger is passing by and he stops at the door.)

| STRANGER | He passed me in the street
and turned in here.
Such despair in his face,
such dread in his gait.
Shall I knock? |

(He goes up to the door and pauses.)

It is not my business.
He is a passer-by.
Is his misery mine?
He might take it amiss
if I knock.
Why should I share his trouble?
What is he to me?
I do not like to interfere.

(He walks up and down.)

| DOLOROUS | Haunting voices from my own heart.
To be alone is danger,
but whom can I importune?
The nearest have all gone. |

(The stranger, who has walked away, comes back and knocks.)

| STRANGER | I went, but I am compelled to come back. |
| DOLOROUS (*within*) | Someone knocks. How can I face
a stranger. It can only be a stranger. |

(Second knock.)

| DOLOROUS | No one would knock but a stranger. |

(Third knock.)

| STRANGER | If no one answers, I shall leave. |

(Dolorous opens the door. The devils go into the

shadows.)

DOLOROUS	Are you looking for me?
STRANGER	We were passers-by. I saw a great need. That is why I am here.
DOLOROUS	I am someone with a ruined life. What shall I do?
STRANGER	If you are ruined in one place, start in another.
DOLOROUS	I belong to this city of Jerusalem.
STRANGER	Break your ties. They are broken already. This city is a place of such order, there is no room to move but out and on, to start again.
DOLOROUS	You do not know my story. You do not realize, until I tell, how I was rejected, how I failed.
STRANGER	I am not concerned with your past. My concern is with your future. You should let go of your misery and start a new life—move on.
DOLOROUS	Where? How?
STRANGER	Jerusalem has rejected you. Leave it behind. Call it a prison fenced in by laws and regulations. Walk out, walk on elsewhere. Do you remember Jericho? That is a place to be at liberty, to forget, to get rid of miseries.
DOLOROUS	I ought to work, to build my life again.
STRANGER	Not so soon. You are not wanted here, by no fault of yours, no doubt. You will be welcome in Jericho. All the more if you have money for lavish spending.
DOLOROUS	I am not without wealth.

What I have shall go with me,
since saving is useless now.
You recommend Jericho?

STRANGER   So full of fascination.
Do not hesitate. Take
the road to Jericho.

DOLOROUS   You knocked. You shared my misery.
You brought a sign of hope.
You deserve more thanks than I can say.

STRANGER   Fare you well.

(*They wave to each other and go off in opposite directions. Dolorous takes to the road, carrying a full basket.*)

DOLOROUS   I travel a lonely road,
why did I not invite a companion?
Since I am among the hills,
I sense danger in the darkness.
Is it good to be alone?

(*He turns anxiously.*)

Have I really left my responsibilities?
It was my choice to take much on myself.
I wished to make life meaningful,
to work for success, to have what I deserve.
But I found failure.
If I am welcome in Jericho,
it will be for my store of money.
I wished to have the wherewithal
to make a true offering to the Angels.
But what have I now to offer?
I am just escaping.

LIGHT DEVIL   Here is devil's work to do.
Here is a man on his own,
without a sense of direction.

DARK DEVIL   Here is devil's work to do.
Here is a man too stupid
to find a sense of direction.

LIGHT DEVIL   You turned to me
when you got above yourself,

escaping alone.

DARK DEVIL | You called on me,
when you took your money
to make friends in Jericho.

(*The demons reappear with the two good-for-nothings,
catching them from behind, whispering in their ears.*)

DEMONS | Do it, down him, work him woe,
take what is his, don't let him go.

TWO-GOOD-FOR-
NOTHINGS | We're not doing anything.
We don't want to do anything.

(*The demons push the good-for-nothings, but they
hold back.*)

TWO GOOD-FOR-
NOTHINGS | Leave us alone. We are idle.
We want to be idle. Go away!

DEMONS | Work woe, we tell you, work woe.

TWO GOOD-FOR-
NOTHINGS | You are pushing and pushing.
It is devil's work.

(*The good-for-nothings rush on Dolorous and knock
him down, scattering his goods.*)

DOLOROUS | Stop, stop, you are thieving.

GOOD-FOR-
NOTHINGS | Shut up. Might is right.
We're miserable, so you shall be miserable
     too.

(*They run off.*)

DEMONS | What we said, they have done.
What misery is now begun!
It's best to run.

(*They both run, leaving Dolorous lying hurt and
helpless.*)

FIRST PASSER-BY
(NEVER-DO-NAUGHT) | How dreadful. Who has done this?
It shouldn't be allowed. It ought to be
     stopped.
But what can I do? One person on his own?
He cannot help himself. I'm very sorry for
     him.

| | Of course, such wickedness should not happen. |
| LIGHT DEVIL | You could not have put it better. Keep out of it. |

(*First passer-by goes off.*)

| SECOND PASSER-BY (NEVER-TRY-NAUGHT) | What is this? It must be an act of robbers. He must have been overpowered. What a shame! It's very wrong. What's to be done? Perhaps he did something to bring it on himself. He took risks or made a mistake. I will call the police; it is their job. |
| DARK DEVIL | You have done the right thing. Make someone else take the trouble. |

(*Second passer-by goes off.*)

| DOLOROUS | Please help me, help me to get up. I am in such pain in all my limbs. |

(*An Angel holding a basket of good deeds comes to look. He turns and beckons. A third passer-by comes in and is led by the Angel to Dolorous.*)

| DOLOROUS (*groaning*) | Help me to get up. I am in such pain. |

(*Merciful bends down and helps Dolorous to sit up.*)

MERCIFUL	How did this happen? Were you set upon? Who did such violence to you?
DOLOROUS	They came upon me from behind. I was alone and could not fight them off. There was more than one—at least two.
MERCIFUL	Have you been robbed?
DOLOROUS	Where is my basket? It has disappeared. Yes, I have been robbed. All that I have is lost.

(He sits with his head in his hands.)

MERCIFUL	What have you lost?

DOLOROUS

There was so much that I strove for.
To have the chance to work hard,
to make something that could be of value,
to have made a place in the world for myself,
to stand for what I believe is right,
all this I have lost. I have nothing, I am
    nothing.
What I founded myself has been ruined by
    others.
Failure, not brought about by me, is my lot.
How can others so ruin one's life?
All the fruits of my efforts are lost.

(The good-for-nothings come past, throwing about the treasures from the basket.)

GOOD-FOR-
NOTHINGS

No use to us, worthless stuff, throw it out.

LIGHT DEVIL

Wastrels, you are good for nothing.

DARK DEVIL

Fools, you are good for nothing.

(The Angels come and gather all up into their baskets.)

ANGELS

We take what was your endeavour.
You will see it no more, but it is not lost.
It is your offering to be taken up to the
    throne,
to be an offering of the Angels to the
    Highest.
Offered for you, when you did not choose to
    offer.

ARCHANGEL

I offer up what was yours; it becomes one
with the history of the world.
It is a promise worthwhile for the future;
it is your life-work offered up,
not to yourself, but to the Divine.
Yours is the new life beginning now.

MERCIFUL

Take what the Earth gives for the

healing of wounds.

(Merciful puts ointment on the wounds of Dolorous.
The Archangel begins to throw shooting stars.
The Angels try to catch the stars.)

ANGELS   Gathering stars from the fields
                where they ripen in the heavens,
                we bring them to heal you.

                (The demons fail to catch the stars.)

MERCIFUL   It all depends on the new start.
                Do not look at your ruined life,
                at all that you have lost
                by malicious interference.
                Look for the open doors, the opportunities.
                What you wished to achieve
                might have become your limitation.
                Now the horizon is far and open.
                You are not bound by what you have done.
                Now you can begin over again.
                Unencumbered you walk on.

DOLOROUS   My strength has gone.

                (The Archangel throws shooting stars. The demons
                cannot catch them.)

DEMONS   Reaching for stars,
                we could use them well;
                dissolving stars,
                they escape from us.

ANGELS   Reaching for stars
                thrown down from Heaven,
                gathering them up
                from the Archangel's hand.

                (An Angel brings a star to Dolorous. He holds it in
                his hand. He begins to get stronger. He stands up by
                himself.)

DOLOROUS   Where shall I go? Where do I begin?

MERCIFUL   Ask your own heart.
                I will walk with you on the first part of the
                    way.

All has disappeared that you meant to take
    with you.
All that you expected from your own efforts
    and aims has gone.
Others took the treasure of your life.
It was thrown away. But Angels gathered it.
In Heaven it thrives for the future.
Seeds of spirit have been planted.
They will ripen and send their fruit
down into the field of Earth.
For man's nature, it is to live here
by what comes from above.
Your failure is a growing force for times
to come. We make offerings without
    knowing
that they were asked for, without intentions.
But there, where we are immortal among
    immortals
we shall know what is intended.
Ask him (*pointing to the Archangel.*)

DOLOROUS

Have you given me strength from Heaven
through the star held in my hands?
For this grace I give thanks.

ARCHANGEL

My treasure in Heaven is the might of iron,
courage-bearing, strength-giving, heart-
    warming.
From the falling stars it descends,
setting off sparks overhead,
sending sparks into human blood.
Courage flares, deeds are dared.
Thought seeks will, will seeks thought.
My grace kindles courage for new hopes,
calling for ventures, for high aims,
calling for the makers of history
to bestir themselves.

DOLOROUS

Will you be my guardian?

ARCHANGEL

As the guardian of mankind,
wielding the iron sword of light,
so shall you know me.
The courageous shall live in my grace.
Do not look back, look forward.

By your aims you shall be known.

(*Merciful walks ahead, Dolorous follows him. The demons rush to meet them, to stop them.*)

LIGHT DEVIL

He will end up among the pleasures of Jericho.

DARK DEVIL

He will end up a dismal failure.

(*The Archangel steps forward and restrains them.*)

ARCHANGEL

Go back, be gone.

(*The good-for-nothings rush in.*)

GOOD-FOR-NOTHINGS

We are miserable; we will make you like us.
We are going back; we take you along.
We will go down together.

(*They pull Dolorous, but Merciful throws them off.*)

MERCIFUL

Let him be. Do not hinder the new beginning.

GOOD-FOR-NOTHINGS

What about us? He is a failure like us.
Who is to be saved?

MERCIFUL

We will forgive you,
for you cannot forgive yourselves.
Forgiven, you will find a new beginning.

ANGELS

Who will give us offerings for our baskets?

STRANGER

I will offer my good intention, my will to help.

MERCIFUL AND DOLOROUS

We will give you acts of forgiveness
born of the grace that flows to Earth from Heaven.

DEMONS

Are we always to be cast out
on whom the doors of Heaven shut?

ARCHANGEL

In the changing history of the world
there are always opportunities
to find redemption,
to raise the fallen.
Those whom you tempted may yet redeem you.

STRANGER   My good intention was not enough.
                            May I be forgiven, who counselled unwisely.

ARCHANGEL   In the sky the stars are shooting,
                            from my hand the stars are falling,
                            courage quickening. Hope reviving,
                            will increasing, thoughts enlivening,
                            catch and hold them, cherishing
                            seeds of light in human keeping,
                            planted where the hearts are warming,
                            grown in hope until the blossoming
                            flowers of light will turn to fruiting,
                            harvest ripe for human offering.
                            Angels, basket-bearers, searching
                            human souls for that beseeching
                            which will make a worthy offering
                            heavenward sent by heartfelt praying.

                            (*The Archangel leads the Angels, with full baskets,
                            away in a procession.*)

8

Christ and the Year

The round of the year is the rhythm in time which is shared by everyone. Spring, summer, autumn, winter enliven the calendar, which has to be renewed each year. It is the background to most of our customs and our undertakings. The conversation in movement between the Sun, the Moon and the Earth gives the round of the year its character and establishes for human beings the world of time. North and South, East and West, the year is shared, but what of the seasons? All the world over the seasons follow each other, but they do not fall at the same time. In this respect the Earth has two halves, a northern and a southern; winter in the North brings summer in the South and spring brings autumn. It has already been observed in Chapter 2 how the movement of the seasons is connected with the activity of the Archangels. In the world of nature the quality of the seasons, even though they follow the same rhythm at opposite times, does not behave in quite the same way. For instance, the sharp distinction between autumn and winter is not the same in the South as it is in the North. Therefore one can suppose that the clarity of the four seasons of the year in the North is reflected more vaguely in the South. Nevertheless, the four seasons are known in their particular version all over the Earth, but at different times.

Old customs of a religious type have reinforced the rhythms in nature and have been shared by human beings. Looking back through history, the fact emerges that in the distant past human life was more connected with nature than it is today. It is clear, for instance, that once upon a time the human day began at sunrise and ended at sunset. In the modern world artificial lighting has changed all that. The connection with the seasons has been changed by methods of heating, so that one can live as if in summer indoors, while in the outside world it is winter. In much earlier times, when what happened in nature strongly affected people, human deeds were held to be much more influential in the natural world than they are today. Two orders of existence have come about, the one belonging to nature and the other to people. But in the ancient world this was not so and people could promote or damage the order of nature by their activities.

Put more simply, religious rites were performed long ago to assist the working of nature. Prayers were chanted to the rising Sun which were thought of and experienced as helping the Sun to rise. Spring was encouraged to come, and winter, inevitably following later, showed to the human soul the contrast between outer and inner. As time went on and minds changed, people farmed the soil, but they were no longer aware of promoting and changing the seasons. They had lost the skill and became victims of the weather, which could be blamed for misfortunes in the raising of crops. Old friendships became a struggle between those holding different points of view. An old gardener used to reply to the garden's owner when he was dissatisfied with the crop: 'I'm not God Almighty—I can't make the weather.' Instead of being nature's helper, he had become a victim, compared with those who knew how to influence conditions in ancient times.

Nowadays a new phase has been reached. Conservation with regard to nature has become the ideal for manifesting good will to the world around. In the meantime, however, the order in nature has become subject to natural laws and fixed. But the Earth has a soul. It has likewise a spiritual history, which is quite mysterious to those accustomed to thinking merely in terms of fixed natural laws alone. Spiritual awareness of the living Earth is the inspiration today for the festivals, which do not come from nature but are implanted into her life. They are spiritual in character, and are celebrated by people aware of the spiritual life within themselves. They add to the rhythm of the year the spiritual purpose which only the human inhabitants of the Earth can give. Such festivals are Christian in character, because the coming into the earthly world of the Son of God has given the life of the Earth new meaning. To the year and the seasons can be added the Christian year and the festivals. The deed of Christ has brought about on Earth a new act of creation, otherwise called the Resurrection. It is performed for the whole world, for the people dwelling on Earth and for the Earth herself, by the guide and leader of earthly history, Christ Himself. The Christian festivals belong to the whole Earth and are received by the Archangels in their different seasons without being brought about by the seasons. They belong to the spiritual unity of the Earth and are accepted in due time into the differing seasonal life in the northern and southern hemispheres. They express the unity which Christ's coming establishes, while the festivals are clothed locally in the garments of the different seasons. The Christian year is the expression of the coming of Christ to the Earth, of the deed of overcoming death, of the purpose for the future.

Since the deeds of Christ are the subject of the festivals in the Christian year, they are not just memorials to what has been done. They are the means by which that which was initiated by Christ in His earthly life can be compared to the sowing of seeds, and which is carried further as the seeds grow into plants. Christ lived on the Earth by occupying the body prepared and offered to Him by Jesus of Nazareth. For a short time the greatest of the gods lived a human life on Earth and took it upon Himself to identify with human history. In an earlier time, the Greeks lived with their gods as visitors from the heavens who could only remain for a short time. But Christ in Jesus was not a visitor. He did not come to depart, but to be transformed in death into the spiritual guide of human history for the future. What He said and did when He lived as Jesus were beginnings which become, and will become further, other deeds of the Son of God made man. The festivals belong to the process of history in which His continuing presence is made known.

At the opening of the Book of Revelation, the story is told of the great vision beheld by John of the resurrected Christ showing the glory of His heavenly nature in human form. John was overwhelmed by its grandeur and fell down on the ground in a deathlike swoon. He was raised up by Christ Himself, in whose presence he saw further visions of the workings of the Risen One in times to come. In other words, that which had overwhelmed him in one great vision became a series of cosmic pictures made comprehensible by being seen one by one. The Christian festivals, following each other in the course of the year, allow the human heart to advance in the whole understanding of Christianity. They call up a process of Christianizing in which everyone may take part at the same time all over the Earth. Differences of language, character, circumstances and point of view are all absorbed into the Christianity which is shared by each one over and above the variations. That this can be so is the effect of Christ's coming from the heavens to the Earth for the sake of the whole of mankind and yet, at the same time, to each Christ-inclined heart.

The year of the Christian festivals begins with Advent, which falls in the month of December. It recalls to our modern mind the long waiting for the coming of the Saviour, the record of which is found in the Old Testament. The Books of the Old Testament repeatedly say that the deed of rescuing mankind from the interference of evil was a matter decided in the heavens. The undertaking is divine, because there could be no human way of solving the problem. The decision is made among the Gods to send their highest one down to share the dilemma into which the human souls had fallen. The origin and beginning of Christianity is the true experience of Advent. It directs human thought and feeling towards the problems of the heavens. It prepares the heart for the revelation of the Christmas festival. The experience of Christmas means to comprehend the reality that the door of Heaven is open, that the Angels come through to prepare the way, that the spirit of Christ, descending from the Sun, begins to enter the lost world of the Earth and make it His temple. The light of the heavens shines in the darkness of Earth. The true purpose of being human begins to quicken again in human souls. The great gift of God in the heavens is given to those on Earth who can receive it in understanding and good will. Night and day, near and far, the circumstances of life on Earth are made holy to refresh those whose hearts can rejoice in holiness. Heaven comes down to Earth in the festival of Christmas.

The following festival is Epiphany. The grace of Christmas is bestowed over the rest of the year. Wise thinking can protect the treasure. It is threatened by the opposition from dark forces in the human heart, illustrated in the historical figure of Herod. He intends to destroy the gift from Heaven. He represents all those who want history to be fashioned out of their earthly aims and their own cleverness. The inspiration of Christ is opposed and threatened. Later in the year, after Epiphany, comes Lent. The human heart and mind sees the revelation of the damage done to human nature by the degrading power of evil. How shall the human being be uplifted by Him who has descended from the heavens?

Lent changes into Easter. The experience of Holy Week makes known the pain and suffering which the Spirit of Christ bears, because He is taking on Himself the tragedy of human history. He is undertaking its utmost consequences that He may struggle to release suffering mankind from the power of death. The festival of Good Friday shows to the heart the real stress and danger of the struggle. There is no foregone conclusion. Christ did not know, the Father in the heavens did not know, whether the mysterious cosmic power of death that had developed on the Earth could be overcome and transformed. The Champion of Mankind had to take the risk. It was taken, it was struggled with, it was overcome. Christ's strength to overcome has worked in the history of mankind ever since the Resurrection on the first Easter morning. Its reality should be felt and understood within the festival of Easter, again and again. The heart can say: 'Do I know, in the mystery of Christmas, who came through the door of Heaven? Do I understand in the mystery of Easter what the divine deed means for all time, which the Son of God performed on Earth through the event of Golgotha? Shall I, in all the years of my life here, ever plumb the depths of understanding to know what the Resurrection truly signifies?'

That which was performed on Earth within the history of mankind was made known to the Company of Heaven through the Ascension. There is no hint in this festival that the risen being of the Christ left the Earth. He became and created in His own being the ladder between Earth and Heaven, which had been foreseen by Jacob in his dream long ago. He remains with the Earth to bring life out of death, to spread light into darkness, to lead mankind into a new fellowship with the Company of Heaven. The next festival, Whitsuntide, demonstrates how the new spiritual forces are brought down the ladder set up by Christ at the

Ascension, to give to human souls a true comprehension of the inspiration of the spirit in man's life on Earth. From Advent until Whitsuntide, the festivals reveal to those who realize it the secret of salvation.

Two festivals complete the Christian year and they relate to the process of accepting the Christian revelation into the human heart. The festival of John the Baptist, at midsummer in the North and midwinter in the South, should call to life in the human heart the insight to comprehend which speaks from the divine spirit in the heavens. Hearing and accepting is the deed of John. The festival of the Archangel Michael wakens in the human mind the willingness to hear his call and to behold the gesture of beckoning which he makes to mankind from the heavens. Courage to know and to accept, to be inspired and to listen to inspiration is required of human souls that they may accompany the Christ from one revelation to another along the path towards what is to come. In some such way as this a person may remind himself in his heart that each Christian festival can bring greater understanding.

Each of the Archangels, from the position through which he is related to the Earth in the course of the Christian year, can cast his light of understanding into the revelation of Christ's coming. When Christmas is experienced in the southern hemisphere in the summer, the Archangel Uriel can teach the secret of the inner light in contrast to the great outer light of the Sun in summer. In the northern hemisphere, the Archangel Gabriel can turn the shining of candlelight in the dark of winter into a parable of Christmas. He can reveal the grace of Epiphany, while waiting for the sunlight to dispel the winter. In the South, the Archangel Uriel can speak of the spiritual fire which kindles enthusiasm and courage when the natural world is exhausted by too much heat. When Easter is encountered in the southern hemisphere in the autumn, the Archangel Michael calls up the courage to face its mystery. But in the North, the Archangel Raphael expounds the secrets of healing to those human souls depressed by the weight of materialistic thought. The four Archangels bring their inspiration around the Earth to quicken the festivals belonging to the whole in ways suited to the seasons over which they preside.

The Archangels are the handmaidens of the festivals, but Christ is their creator. Out of the deed performed by the Son of God for mankind and for the Earth, Christianity continues to shine and to evolve. It is not at an end, because Christ's working continues. It inspires the festivals and makes clear to Christian hearts that what has begun will have a future, what has been undertaken will persist towards fulfilment.

Russian Legend

On the field of Golgotha, nailed to the Cross, with arms spread wide, with blood-red wounded hands, Christ hung on the holy Cross in the middle of the Earth, raising up through Himself the work of His divine hands: this world of the four dimensions, the length, the breadth, the height and the depth. The Angels passing up and down from Heaven gathered together in companies. The powers of Heaven bowed down before the suffering He had taken upon Himself.

Praised be thy long suffering, Lord.

The mighty beings of the heavens, all nine ranks—Angels, Archangels, Archai, the Powers, the Mights, the Rulers, Thrones, Cherubim and Seraphim—stood before Him, before the Throne of Glory in their ranks, ascending and descending. And the dead rose out of the graves, came near to the Cross and bowed themselves before His suffering which brings healing.

Praised be thy long suffering, Lord.

The two robbers nailed to the cross died in agony, in the dull heaviness of death. Their thoughts died, their shattered reason dissolved, darkness blinded the eyes of their senses and their spirit. Their hearts melted and they besought: 'Gracious Lord God have mercy on me who am fallen.' Spreading out her arms crosswise to the Son, whose arms were spread out on the Cross, the holy Mother of God sinks down by the Cross. The sword of sorrow pierces through her heart; her torn heart is baptized with the baptism of tears.

Praised be thy long suffering, Lord.

Three stars like three candles of God shine out of the darkness from the Virgin Mother who once bore in a wonderful manner Him who is the light and salvation of the world.

Where the sun rises, twelve doors were opened, twelve others in the West, twelve on the sea. From all the paths of the upper and lower heavens mighty beings came to the Cross. Two Angels brought the old man, supporting him under the arms—the venerable, infirm Adam, the first of creation—and stood him before the countenance of the Lord. With sunken head Christ hung upon the Cross for all to worship Him, for the forgiveness of sins of everyone who through faith ascends to Heaven. He drank bitter gall, the One of the beginning, who is without beginning and end, who is eternal. And a voice came from the Cross: 'For thy sake and for the sake of thy children am I come to Earth, from Heaven down to the Cross, and nailed here. Today I fulfil the covenant: I forgive thee thy guilt.' And Adam sighed: 'So was thy will, so was thy will, Lord my God.'

Praised be thy long suffering, Lord.

The Angels, the heavenly hosts, rejoiced, praising Christ who redeemed with blood the sins of the firstborn. The dark nights are past, the woe is over. And they rose from the Cross in awe and joy up to the Heaven of Heavens, to the Throne of Glory, praising Christ to the Heavenly Father.

Praised be thy long suffering, Lord.

The heavenly hosts ascended to the throne of God, praising the divine suffering. But one of the Angels, glorious of countenance, stood before the Cross motionless. He alone gazed in silence at Christ. 'How can it be! God's beloved Son, the brother, the King of Heaven, the Creator of Earth and Heaven, is sold for thirty pieces of silver, hangs on the Cross, suffers, covered in blood from head to foot, and no one comes to help. He is left alone defenceless.' The Angel saw no one but Christ, gazed only on Him. He could not be quieted; his fingers were twisted into each other in torment, and smoke, like the blue smoke from the censer, rose from between the pointed joints. His spear shimmered white in his hands and his stormy wings, blue as thunder-clouds, were loud with anger like those of an eagle. Motionless, silent, he could not, he would not, see Christ on the Cross. All the mighty beings of Heaven looked at each other in wonder and besought the Angel to ascend to the Throne of Glory. But his heart burned, a thought flamed up in the burning heart: he alone can and will and must rise up to aid and protect. He can bring vengeance on the towns and villages, destroy the fields, hills and forests and blot out the whole world and the crown of the Sun as the penalty for the Cross and the agony.

Praised be thy long suffering, Lord.

Alone, motionless, in silence he stood in flames before the Cross, the avenger, the victor over the enemy, the Archangel Michael. In snow-white whirling mass, the heavenly hosts ascended above the circle of the stars towards the Throne to sing praises of the Cross. And Christ commanded the Angel to ascend to Heaven to leave the Cross.

'Fulfil the Law.'

But faithful to the Cross the Angel stood and could not go away. 'Lord, thou seest I cannot endure your crucifixion.' But God commanded the Angel to withdraw.

'Fulfil the Law.'

But the Angel did not move. He stood firm and immovable, faithfully in front of the Cross. 'Lord how shall I go?' And for the third time a voice came from the Cross commanding the Angel to ascend to Heaven.

'Fulfil the Law.'

Shadows shuddered over the pale head. Quivering, the Angel took one step from the Cross, then he suddenly stopped and turned. Dark shadows whirled around him. The stormy wings shook like those of an eagle. To see the suffering, to have the power to turn it aside and not be allowed to do it. 'Do not require it of me, O Lord. Thou seest my glowing heart, thou knowest my love. Thy Law, thy word, thy will, I cannot resist. My love I cannot wipe out.'

The fire of love was so great, the suffering so bitter, all thoughts and all ways of the heart were so aflame, the Angel could not give in, could not fulfil the command of God. He loosed his fingers and the flame, blue hot, living, left his hand. The seven spheres of Heaven drew together and the Earth shuddered. In the roar of the fearful trumpet of woe, the four winds rose up from the four spaces of the heavens. They roared from East and West, from North and South. They could not stop; madly they rushed into the sea so that it towered up and threatened to drown the whole Earth. The pillars of Hell were shaken.

But in thunder, tumult and havoc, suffering grows sharper, wrath knows no relief. The Angel threw his spear into the darkness of the Earth, the place of fear, torment and desolation. The agonized heart beat helplessly. Cleaving the darkness like lightning, the spear struck the Temple, cut through the dome, broke into the courtyard and split the wall into two from top to bottom. The Angel tore the curtain of the Temple in two, for witness to the sons of men of the pain on the Cross that they should behold and know.

And in the same hour Christ lifted up His voice, praising the Father God, and the only begotten Son gave up the ghost, the great Light Angel, the Word of God to overcome death in death.

Praised be thy long suffering and thy power, Lord and God.

9

Christ and the Future

The festivals are a series of spiritual events celebrating the mystery of Christ, performed on Earth for the Father in Heaven. They are continuing events, taking further into history the original deeds of Christ when He lived a human life in the body of Jesus. The divine being of Christ descended into this body when John the Baptist performed the act of baptism in the River Jordan. He passed out of this body again through the death on the Cross on Golgotha. In the act of overcoming death, He created His own spiritual physical body and lives on as the guide and leader of mankind into the future process of history. The Resurrection is an event that continues to evolve into the ages of time, creating out of itself the future existence of man on Earth. Rightly celebrated, the festivals express and create the process of becoming and growing into the future.

In the course of the year the cycle of festivals begins with Advent, which prepares for the central event of Christmas. It is the time for experiencing something of human history as a whole. Its theme is that which has happened through the creation of man, what has developed through the interference of evil and what has to be overcome if man's nature and destiny shall be led into the creative future. Such an experience is given expression in the symbol of the Advent wreath. The wreath is round and whole and decorated with four candles which will be lighted one after the other through the four weeks of Advent.

Christmas itself is an event of cosmic history, taking place on the Earth for the whole of mankind. It celebrates the descent from the heavens of the Son of God, who is transformed into the Son of Man for the spiritual purpose of rescuing mankind for the future. On Christmas night and during the Twelve Holy Nights, the gift of the heavens to the Earth is celebrated. The future of mankind depends upon the salvation brought to the Earth by the coming of Christ. The birth of the Child speaks in a picture of the rebirth of man's divine being, which has become entangled and spoilt by the interference of evil powers. But mankind was born from the heavens with a divine purpose. The twofold powers of evil wish to divert the purpose into something of their own. In the light brought down at Christmas, the event of salvation begins. Heaven-born, this light shines into the darkness, which is a spiritual reality for the whole Earth. The festival of Epiphany following on Christmas allows the light to be born into the Earth itself, into the striving history of mankind, which has become the true purpose of life on Earth. The light of Christmas descends and remains. In the course of the year's round, the festival following will be Lent. It prepares for the next festival of salvation, for Easter, with its consequences, the festivals of Ascension and Whitsuntide. The experience of Lent awakens in the human heart knowledge of the deeper meaning of death and decadence. The picture can be realized of what man's future would be if these were not truly experienced. The inner powers of the soul need to be prepared to meet the challenge of Resurrection. The danger and sorrow of Good Friday is to be felt in the human heart, because it is an experience of the Christ, who, being the Son of God, risked the encounter with the power of death and was able to emerge triumphant out of the struggle. The risk was real and within it was prepared, through suffering, the strength to overcome and to carry the being of man onwards to a new future. In a sense, Resurrection is beyond our human comprehension, but the celebration of a true Easter festival will bring mankind over the whole Earth into the process of rebirth.

What happens through Easter is still beyond our comprehension; it is still a promise of the future. But with each coming again of the festival, human hearts must take a step forward towards the realization of what is to come. Christ achieved the overcoming of death and the Resurrection that the mystery shall become the true theme of human history. That which historically took place on Earth in our history was witnessed by men and women who were present at the turning point of time. It had to be made known further to the Company of Heaven, from whom Christ had descended. This was done at the festival of Ascension. The Risen Christ expanded His presence into the realms beyond the Earth. The Resurrection became known to the heavenly company when Christ showed them His risen nature. It is the part of the mystery of earthly life which is shared with the heavens, because the Risen One, without leaving the Earth, could reveal the truth of Resurrection that had been established when He rose out of death.

Whitsuntide is the festival of understanding. Christ's Resurrection has changed the evolution of mankind, has opened a way towards the ascension of man into the community of the heavens. The Holy Spirit descended so that human hearts could be enlightened with understanding of the significance of what was taking place. It brings another kind of communion. The event of death overcome is a divine deed done on the Earth. Man has to become a part of the happening, has to triumph over his ignorance, finding that he can understand, in some measure at least, the mystery of his own uprising, which is made real to him by grace. The Holy Spirit descended at the first Whitsuntide to become the companion of mankind on the way towards resurrection. The event completes that which is begun at Easter. There are still two other festivals in the Christian year, which have the effect of completing the cycle. The one is the festival of man taken up into the history made by Christ. John the Baptist represents the human soul absorbed into the process of resurrection, both as a prophet and a martyr, in what is performed by God on Earth. The last festival is that of the Archangel Michael and it celebrates the cooperation between man and the Angels in preparing the future, which will bring the life of humanity into companionship with those who enact history in the heavens.

Each of the festivals can speak in symbols of its character. Advent has already been spoken of with the picture of the wreath representing the whole year, and also the cycle of festivals in the Christian year. Christmas carries the symbol of the candle burning and shining in the dark, or burning and shining within, in contrast to the strong shining of the Sun outside. The symbol of Epiphany is the Star showing the way through the heavens. In Lent, the darkness of the fallen world speaks of the threat of living cut off from the true light of the heavens. Easter is the festival of the Sun, illuminating and accompanying the human journey through this world below. Whitsuntide carries the symbol of the flames. St John's Tide is expressed in the fire answering the light of the Sun, and Michaelmas is represented by the Archangel with the sword of light.

The Christian Community, which was founded in modern times with the help of Rudolf Steiner, has been entrusted with the care of the new sacraments. In the Communion service entitled 'The Act of Consecration of Man', there are prayers describing the experience of the festivals as they come round in the course of the Christian year. As the words of these sacraments are never put into print, but are reserved for the experience of the spoken word, they cannot be quoted here. But the vestments used by the celebrants vary in colour according to the festival. In Advent they are a strong blue, at Christmas white, and in Epiphany purple. In Lent the vestments are black. At Easter the colour changes to red, which is still so at Ascension. At Whitsun and also during the Festival of St John they are white. At Michaelmas they become pink. During these festivals certain forces of the human soul are called up in relation to the prayers, which are not quoted, but can be heard by those who attend the services. The festivals are marked by the qualities of heart which should be called forth. In Advent, the emphasis is upon hoping, at Christmas upon knowing, upon that kind of faith which is also knowledge. Epiphany is the festival understood by the heart which is aware of receiving grace with gratitude. The dark time of Lent calls up in the heart sorrowful anticipation. It is a mood of questioning, which is answered at Easter with the promise of consolation and comfort. Ascension calls upon the power of thinking to rise to true Imagination. At Whitsuntide, the healing power of the spirit works to uplift the longings of the soul. The festival of St John's Tide calls up thanksgiving in the human heart and Michaelmas demands the strength of courage. A true celebration of these festivals from year to year strengthens the spiritual qualities in the inner life.

Bible readings, which are adjusted artistically to the nature of the festivals, not only reflect what has already happened in the past but the qualities of the spirit which are rightly related to the substance of the festivals. Advent is the time when what comes out of the future into the present is revealed. There belong to it all those prophecies found in the Gospels, of which Chapter 21 of St Luke's Gospel is an example. What is coming next in the history of Christianity? The birth of the Child has already happened. He grew up and became the bearer of the Spirit of Christ on Earth. What this means is still to be understood more deeply. Nevertheless, the next event in the history of Christ is not a repetition of His coming down to Earth, but His coming into revelation in the heights beyond the Earth, in the sphere to which the clouds are the doorstep. Such is the Christian vision expressing the meaning of Advent.

The stories for the festival of Christmas are twofold. In the Gospel of St Luke we hear of the homeless parents coming to Bethlehem, of the Child born in the stable with the ox and ass beside him and of the shepherds called from the fields by the Angels. As Christmas turns into Epiphany, the story from St Matthew's Gospel appears, describing the Wise Men from afar, who discover the Star which shines by night as the Sun by day. Guided by the Star they find their way to Bethlehem to see the Child guarded by father and mother. These stories are not the same, but bring with them the twofold vision of Christmas. In the transition between Christmas and Easter, the stories appear in Lent which indicate the qualities needed today to appreciate the new birth of fallen mankind. These include a new awareness of the inner life in the mind as compared with the outer, and the longing for new strength in the inner life to prepare for the spiritual happening of Easter. At that festival there will be time to think of passages from the conversations recorded in St John's Gospel in connection with the Last Supper. These are, in truth, conversations that extend all through the experience of the forty days of the Resurrection, offering to the attentive heart the deep meanings behind the accounts of meetings with the Risen Christ. Behind all that is said in the Gospels stands the profound questioning of the human mind: how can I through the years come to a true understanding of the fact that Christ, having passed through death, could show to mankind the way towards the future through the Resurrection?

The story of John the Baptist speaks in various ways of how he was called by the Father God to take part in carrying out the divine intention for man's earthly life. The pictures of the Archangel Michael, which are most plainly told in the Book of Revelation of St John, reveal the Archangel facing intently the powers of evil that threaten to distort the history of the world. Throughout Michaelmas and afterwards, the most impressive stories are found in the Book of Revelation. The future will not be man-made; it will be fashioned in the heavens to be reflected on the Earth. In the last book of the Bible, the events continue to the end of time. History changes, experiences become different, freer from the intentions inspired by the interests of this world. The heavens and the Earth are and will be coming nearer together. Human thinking will need to aspire more and more heavenward. The concerns of Angels and Archangels will become more obvious for human minds. A great future opens up before our thought, for heavenly interests will become as decisive as earthly ones.

One of the last pictures in the Bible is that of the marriage between the heavenly bridegroom and the earthly bride. What has been separated must be joined together. What belongs to the Earth must be lifted up to the heavens. What belongs to time must be touched by Eternity. Such considerations belong to the experience of the religious mind. Is it only in terms of natural science that we see facts? If we look for realities in the time to come, it will be necessary to look with the eye of faith at that which is being created since the Resurrection for the future. Does faith show us reality of another kind? Is faith of this kind more important? Is our Christian, spiritual life more truly related to the realities of existence than we can understand at the present time?

The Prodigal Son

SCENE 1

At the entrance to a house within a courtyard and built in the style and proportions used by Fra Angelico, two servants appear. Their costumes are of a simple style.

1st SERVANT   Where is the master of the house?
                     He was always here
                     at the usual time
                     until now—

2nd SERVANT   Our fellow servants
                     will have gone to the fields
                     and begun the day's work.
                     But we must wait here
                     to receive our instructions.

1st SERVANT   Is something new in the air?

2nd SERVANT   The master went with heavy step
                     in recent days.

1st SERVANT   Can you foresee his plans?

2nd SERVANT   His mind is as wide
                     as his great estates
                     I see with a servant's eye.

1st SERVANT   Far stretch the lands
                     of which he is the lord
                     whom we serve through the seasons,
                     so far that their bounds
                     I have never yet seen.

2nd SERVANT   To strange places afar
                     have I travelled with him
                     when he was concerned
                     to know for himself

the state of his lands.
To the utmost limit
we never came.

1st SERVANT   He keeps his wealth wisely
and looks for the thriving
of all in his care.
His rule is well ordered,
his law firm established
in great things and small.

2nd SERVANT   He knows well the strength
of order maintained
of laws rightly kept.
But he understands more
the flash of new thought,
the aim beyond plan,
the purpose unknown.

1st SERVANT   Justice and right
are upheld by his hand.
What he ordains
his servants perform.

2nd SERVANT   Mercy and grace
he freely can give.
More he performs
than his servants foresee.

(*The elder son enters.*)

ELDER SON   Where is my Father?
He will surely come with me
away to the fields.

SERVANTS   We wait for him to come,
He is still within doors.

ELDER SON   Why such delay?
The usual hour is past
when the work of the day should begin.
Enquire when he comes.

(*1st servant goes out.*)

ELDER SON   See how high the Sun climbs
(*to 2nd servant*)   on his daily path and we are still idle.

(*The servant returns with the Father.*)

FATHER

The day brings forth the glory of God;
the Sun declares it through the heavens.
Star unto star in answer calls
and from the depths sounds back the echo.
Blest be the light of day for creation.
Blest be the life that quickens the creatures.
Blest be the labour my son of your strength.

ELDER SON

Blest be the day for you my Father.
The time for work has come.
The servants wait and we should go.

FATHER

What shall be done today?

ELDER SON

Wide are the fields of the stars
where the world seeds quicken
that are sown in the heavens.
Many are the servants sent
to till those fields with care
and each in his skill and strength
is fit for the work he plies.
There the harvest is grown
that is reaped for the sake of the world.
There creation continues
that the universe may endure.
There life is born out of life
that the works of God may not cease.
Shall not the elder son
go up and down in the fields
and with the voice of the Father
speak to the servants at work?
Who shall care for the order
and working of all things but he?

(*Chorus of servants in question and answer.*)

1st SERVANT

What shall the harvest be
that is reaped in the fields of the Moon?

2nd SERVANT

When the wisdom of God
is sown in the fields of the Moon
the power to give form is brought forth
that works in the world's becoming.

1st SERVANT

What shall the harvest be

that is reaped in Mercury's fields?

2nd SERVANT	When the wisdom of God is sown in Mercury's fields the power to heal is brought forth that flows where sickness is wielding.
1st SERVANT	What shall the harvest be That is reaped in the fields of Venus?
2nd SERVANT	When the wisdom of God is sown in the fields of Venus the power of love is brought forth that one to the other attracts.
1st SERVANT	What shall the harvest be that is sown in the fields of the Sun?
2nd SERVANT	When the wisdom of God is sown in the fields of the Sun, the glory of light is brought forth that in beauty creates through the world.
1st SERVANT	What shall the harvest be that is sown in the fields of Mars?
2nd SERVANT	When the wisdom of God is sown in the fields of Mars the power to speak is brought forth that utters the word from within.
1st SERVANT	What shall the harvest be that is sown in Jupiter's fields?
2nd SERVANT	When the wisdom of God is sown in Jupiter's fields, the power of thought is brought forth that gives to the world its meaning.
1st SERVANT	What shall the harvest be that is sown in Saturn's fields?
2nd SERVANT	When the wisdom of God is sown in Saturn's fields recollection within is brought forth that lets inwardness live in the world.
ELDER SON	Who shall watch the harvest? Who shall measure the corn?

Who shall care for the keeping
and the rightful sharing
of the gathered grain?
Who but the son and the Father
shall give heed to the whole?

FATHER

My son, you are regent
through the extent of my lands.
You are sent to uphold
the rule of right order
and the might of my law.

ELDER SON

To this I am bound, my Father,
by the whole will of my nature.
Let us go at once to the fields.
Or must I go in your stead?

FATHER

Go alone, my son,
The servants will hear
that you speak with my voice.
I must stay here
for the sake of your brother.
He is young and begins to ask
what shall become of him.

ELDER SON

Shall he not go with me
and learn the care of your lands?

FATHER

To each of my sons is due
his share in our wealth,
his task in the whole
and his way of life.
You have what is yours.
Go now my son,
and may your toil be blest
and the harvest thrive.

ELDER SON

As you will, my Father.
At evening I shall be here again.

(*He goes away. The younger son comes in.*)

YOUNGER SON

He strides on ahead
and will not turn at my call.
There is no time to wait,
I must be ready and off.
He should have stayed for me.

FATHER	He cannot know that you will go before evening. He could not imagine a wish like that you uttered today. You have outgrown boyhood and are filled with desire to find the unknown. When your brother reached manhood he found contentment in the daily cares of our estates. Such work could be yours.
YOUNGER SON	It is enough, my Father, that one of your sons will stay at your side to uphold in all things your order and farseeing rule. But I long to leave home and the shelter of your domain, to go where my endeavour will shape my way of existence. Set me free to depart.
FATHER	You are weary of home, my son, eager to be away, longing for the new world beyond the old boundaries. What do you hope for there? For liberty not known within my ordered domain? My son, you are seeking danger.
YOUNGER SON	Shall the son be restrained by the fears of the father?
FATHER	Not from fear of disaster have I given my warning, but to remind you that you seek without understanding that which you cannot know. But seek you shall and alone.
YOUNGER SON	May I go with your good will?
FATHER	It must be so.

This world where my word holds good
and my law is always upheld
shall not be the whole of existence.
The unknown from the known is divided
and out of the far unknown
the germ of life shall be quickened
for which the universe waits.
In the age-old order of all things
shall the seed of freedom be planted
that what shall be evolve from what is.

YOUNGER SON　　What is this new thing freedom?

FATHER　　In the far unknown it is hidden
where danger is constantly lurking.
Out of the risk it shall grow
that the World-Father shall bear.

YOUNGER SON　　What risk is this?

FATHER　　Shall I count what is given you
as a heavenly inheritance?
Shall I reckon the wealth of worlds
with which you shall be endowed?
These shall not be counted
compared with the risk of my son,
who goes he knows not whither
to danger he cannot foresee
for a purpose he cannot imagine.
You yourself are the risk, my child.

YOUNGER SON　　Am I not always your son
having around me your blessing
to keep and protect me?

FATHER　　You are bound to a country far off
where all that you have and are
is staked for an unknown gain.
My servants are now at the door
bringing the share you inherit
from the wealth of the heavens,
the share of the younger son.

1st SERVANT　　Here is your portion
drawn from the wealth of the Moon.

2nd SERVANT　　The Moon bequeaths silver

to have, to hold and to use.

1st SERVANT	Here is your portion drawn from the wealth of Mercury.
2nd SERVANT	Mercury bequeaths quicksilver to have, to hold and to use.
1st SERVANT	Here is your portion drawn from the wealth of Venus.
2nd SERVANT	Venus bequeaths copper to have, to hold and to use.
1st SERVANT	Here is your portion drawn from the wealth of the Sun.
2nd SERVANT	The Sun bequeaths gold to have, to hold and to use.
1st SERVANT	Here is your portion drawn from the wealth of Mars.
2nd SERVANT	Mars bequeaths iron to have, to hold and to use.
1st SERVANT	Here is your portion drawn from the wealth of Jupiter.
2nd SERVANT	Jupiter bequeaths tin to have, to hold and to use.
1st SERVANT	Here is your portion drawn from the wealth of Saturn.
2nd SERVANT	Saturn bequeaths lead to have, to hold and to use.
SERVANTS (*together*)	Child of the universe endowed with life that flows from starry worlds, within yourself their essences unite into one form. Rich with the wealth of worlds depart to the unknown. Never forget from whence you have your birth, Never forget of whom you are the child.

FATHER
(*giving to him a circlet of stars*)

Your head was formed
when all the stars in chorus
sounded their music.
The image of the universe itself
is mirrored in its round.
This crown of stars
I place upon your head,
that, in the distant land
the star-bred wisdom
in your thinking shine.

(*He puts a golden garment on the son.*)

Your heart was forged
out of the fiery Sun,
fired with a golden glow
and set to beat
to the world rhythm.
The golden garment
shall be your clothing
that the Sun-born gold
in your feeling shine.

(*He gives him shoes.*)

Your limbs were shaped
by the power of the Moon
and made in the image
evolved by the stars
of the twelvefold circle
creating together.
Put shoes on your feet
that their forming power
in your willing work.

YOUNGER SON

The strangers whom I meet
will know at sight
that of a worthy house I am the son,
so rich am I with this inheritance.
Now, with your blessing, Father,
I will depart.

(*Another figure, like that of a brother, appears and stands behind the son. He is silent.*)

FATHER

The servants shall go

some way along your road.
My son, on a strange adventure
greater than you foresee
you are setting out this day.
To a far country alone
with the risk of everything
you have and are, you go
for a world purpose hid
far beyond your present mind.
My blessing shall be like a cloak
wrapt closely around you.
My love shall be a light
that shines on your distant way.
You are my well loved son,
my fatherhood shall endure
though distance, sin and death
shall come between us both.
Your sonship shall remain
beyond the ages.

YOUNGER SON

I shall not forget
to show myself your son.
Farewell, my Father.

FATHER
(*makes a gesture of blessing*)

Farewell my son.

(*The silent brother and the Father look after him as he goes, following the servants, without looking back.*)

SCENE 2

In the far country the son is lying asleep on the ground. A light devil and a dark devil (a luciferic and an ahrimanic being) stand, the first one to the front of the stage, the other to the back.

LIGHT DEVIL

There was war in Heaven.
Those who would keep in one
in the great, undivided whole
the will of the gods,
one Godhead, one purpose, one will,
fought with those who had dared
to assert that other will
of selfhood strong in itself

to oppose and convert the plan.

DARK DEVIL

There was war in Heaven.
Those who wielded the might
of darkness and carried it far
into the spheres of the light
with the power of the will against
them were cast down from the heights,
dragging with them this other
whose light shone false
from his heavenly throne.

LIGHT DEVIL

In this country far off
from the realm of God's rule
my power shall work at will.
Where the presence divine
has been withheld
I will shape a world of my own.

DARK DEVIL

You dispute this realm with me.
By yourself you soon would dissolve
this world to an airy cloud.
My strength maintains it as real
and fit for us both to work.

LIGHT DEVIL

My kingdom shall surely prevail
but I wish not to dwell there alone.
Some creature to be mine own
I desire to entice at my will.

DARK DEVIL

It is known that the younger son
has set out from the Father's house
well endowed with his share of its wealth.
Stupid enough he will be
to bend to the purpose I plan,
but you shall entice him first,
since the lust of pride prepares
the heart for the itch of greed.

(*A servant appears sent from the Father's house.*)

SERVANT

You princes who seek below
the realms you have lost above,
hear the message I bring from Him
whose fatherly care extends
from end to end of the world.

The younger son is sent out
alone from the Father's house
to this far country where you
without hindrance your will can unfold.
He is sent to fulfil in the future
a secret purpose divine
still unborn from the mind of God.
He will not be kept from temptation.
The risk is already accepted
but in no wise is it intended
that he come to serve your will.
In this world he shall find the fulfilment
of other ends than yours.

LIGHT DEVIL

This world shall be *mine*.
The spheres of Heaven are His.
Who comes here serves *me*.

SERVANT

Your wisdom may not survey
what is still intended.
God's will shall still be wrought
in this forsaken world.

DARK DEVIL

Let the son come.
What is intended
can be turned to other uses.
Where is he?

SERVANT

He lies here asleep and is dreaming
of the home that he left so lately.

LIGHT DEVIL

Poor child, he must certainly waken.

DARK DEVIL

Poor fool, he looks helpless enough.

SERVANT

To return whence I came is my duty.
Remember what I have told you.
The risk is already taken
but his purpose may never be yours.

(*He goes off. The two devils approach the sleeping son.*)

LIGHT DEVIL

He is here. He must be awakened
to behold the world he inhabits.

DARK DEVIL

He is well endowed. From us shall he learn
to make use of the gifts he brings.

(*At this moment the silent brother comes in and stands on the opposite side of the son to the devils. He remains there until they leave.*)

LIGHT DEVIL   I will give him what he needs
for his new life.

(*He touches the eyes of the son.*)

And when you look
beautiful and good shall be
what eyes shall see.

(*He waves his arm between the son and the world around. The light devil touches the hands of the son.*)

You will work outwards
from the centre of self.

DARK DEVIL   And when you work
substantial and real shall be
what hands shall touch.

(*He stamps and makes a gesture of compressing and making firm what is around. The son begins to waken. The dark devil pulls the light devil towards the back of the stage out of sight.*)

DARK DEVIL   Let him learn to enjoy the world
before he learns who rules here.

(*The light devil goes and stands behind the son and opens his arms upwards over him.*)

LIGHT DEVIL   I will give you all the world
when you acknowledge me.

(*The dark devil beckons from behind.*)

DARK DEVIL   I will make this world my own
and you shall worship me.

(*Both devils disappear and the son wakes up gradually without seeing them. The silent brother leaves too.*)

YOUNGER SON   Where am I?
Was it a dream
when I thought myself
at home in my Father's house?
Or am I dreaming now

in this strange new world?
Which is sleeping?
Which is waking?

(*He gets up and begins to look about him.*)

Almost I have forgotten
how I came here.
Once—was it long ago?—
I resolved to leave home
and my Father blessed me
and another stood at his side.
Was it really myself
who wished for that departure?
Why do I not remember
how I came to this place?
Nothing here is familiar.
All is unknown.

(*He goes round looking in all directions with wonder.*)

This is the unknown world I desired
but how strange to be here alone.
I am quite, quite alone.
Never before was I far from my Father,
and servants were always at hand.
Now there is none but myself.
The unknown creeps up full of dread.
Who will answer when I call out
in the fear of loneliness?

(*A gnome peeps out.*)

GNOME   What makes you sure
                    that you are alone in the world,
                    stupid one?
                    I was peering at your back
                    all the time.

YOUNGER SON   Who are you?
                    Where do you come from?

GNOME   So stupid that you cannot guess.
                    Where have you sprung from, thickheaded one?

YOUNGER SON   From my Father's house.

GNOME   So you are one of the sons,

the small one grown bigger.
What are you doing here?
This is not the place for the sons.

YOUNGER SON   My Father agreed to my going
                     and gave me a share of his wealth.

GNOME   Let us see what you bring.

*(The gnome looks at the shoes and the garment, and begins
to show excitement over the crown. But when he sees the
metals, he becomes fervent.)*

Grand and glorious
is the treasure.
Great and generous
is the measure
that your Father gave.
Magic mighty
power portentous
you shall wield
in Earth's domain.

YOUNGER SON   What do you mean?
                     Is the treasure for use?
                     I guarded it safely in awe of my Father.
                     That it had use I never knew.

GNOME   Thickheaded one!
(laughing in scorn)   They dispatched you here
                     without lending the lore
                     you would need on the way.

(A sylph comes hastening past.)

GNOME   Hie, flibbety gibbet there!
                     What did I tell you!
                     He is come. He is come.

(The sylph swerves back again.)

SYLPH   Are you calling me, wisehead?
                     What news have you now?

GNOME   I knew he was coming,
                     and now he is here
                     but stupid and helpless
                     past all belief.

SYLPH   Poor creature, so helpless!
                 How lovely his clothing.
                 The stars gave his crown,
                 the Sun gave his gown,
                 the Moon gave his shoes.
                 O heavenly creature,
                 why be exiled to Earth?

YOUNGER SON   I journeyed here from afar,
                 I know not how,
                 and have forgotten why.
                 Now at least I am not alone.
                 Tell me who and what you are.

SYLPH   We nourish, we cherish
                 the increase of the fruit.
                 We lighten, we ripen
                 the seed with the blossom.
                 We hunger, we yearn
                 for the light of the air.
                 We fashion, we form
                 with the forces they bear.

GNOME   We tramp and we tread
                 where the metals are threading
                 their way through the rocks.
                 We pull and we push
                 when the seedlings are growing
                 up out of the ground.
                 We hear and we hold
                 what the heavens are telling
                 in depths of the Earth.

YOUNGER SON   Whom do you serve then?

GNOME AND SYLPH The Father in Heaven
                 has appointed our place,
                 fashioned our nature
                 and set us our duties.
                 Although we live here
                 in this country afar
                 we still are his servants
                 and know His regard.
                 Since you are His son
                 you also we serve.

	In willing devotion we take you as lord.
YOUNGER SON	My Father has sent these servants ahead to help me. How great has been His care!
GNOME TO SYLPH	Now he has arrived and intends to remain there is no escape.
SYLPH	How long must I be here when I yearn to be away. The dark always threatens but I flee to the light.

(She disappears in flight.)

YOUNGER SON	Why has she gone?
GNOME	We serve as our duty but we long to be free from the world where we feel the forces of matter pressing us hard.
YOUNGER SON	But surely there is much to enjoy here.
GNOME	You have much wealth and far too little sense. I will show you how to use it. You should unite with the Earth the treasure you bring and receive it again to use.

(An undine comes in with a floating-swimming motion.)

UNDINE	Has he come? I hear he has come.

(She encircles the son inspecting him.)

	If only you had not come we had not needed to stay.
YOUNGER SON	Who are you? Are you also a servant of my Father?
UNDINE	We are swirling and whirling in all that is growing. We are changing, transmuting in all that is living.

We seize on the substance
that to form is turning
and dissolve into process
of endless becoming.

YOUNGER SON   What marvellous servants
are at work in this world.

UNDINE   The power to transform
to dissolve, to refashion
shall be yours, if you use it.

*(She goes away as quickly as she came. A salamander
appears with great coloured wings.)*

SALAMANDER   The sylphs are saying
that the younger son is here.

(He flies up to the son and gazes at him.)

Yes, he is here.
By the stars round his head,
by the golden garment
I see he is heaven-sent.

YOUNGER SON   Are you also a servant?

SALAMANDER   We descend from the heights
with the life that shall quicken
new seeds in the plants.
We fashion their forms
in the warmth that from Heaven
streams down to the Earth.
We go up and down
from the heights to the depths,
from the depths to the heights.

YOUNGER SON   Then you know the way from that world to
this?

SALAMANDER   Never forget down here below
that you came from above,
that you live by favour of Heaven.

(He flies away again.)

GNOME   Now come with me,
I will show you the wonders of Earth.
You shall learn how to use

	the fortune you bring.
YOUNGER SON	What must I do?
GNOME	The sevenfold treasure
	must be laid in the ground
	and given to the Earth.
	So it will become wealth
	for your use and your gain.
	You are so stupid,
	who can tell how you will waste it!
YOUNGER SON	Already I begin to see with new eyes,
	to find wonders with every look.
	My Father's house seems like a dream
	that fades as I awaken.
	This place is my real inheritance
	where I shall begin to exist
	in the reality for which I yearned.

(He and the gnome go off together. The dark devil passes across the back of the stage following them. The light devil comes to the front.)

LIGHT DEVIL	He has now awakened
	and comes into his own.
	The world lies before him
	to see and enjoy.
	We shall share the wealth
	that he brings with him,
	for we gave him sight
	and the lust of enjoyment.

(He follows the others.)

SCENE 3

The gnome pushes on a table and brings bowls. The sylph brings fruit and food and wine.

GNOME	He was stupid from the start
(grumbling to himself)	but ignorant more than anything.
	He was beginning to learn
	and to do what I told him.
	But now it's sheer folly!
	Oh the waste of it!

SYLPH

Poor creature, so foolish.
How can he forget
that the Sun and the Moon
and the stars in the heavens
have brought forth the riches
that here he is squandering.
What if the Father
should hear of this wasting!

GNOME

When he came
we knew by each feature
that he was the son.
Then they got hold of him
too daft to know them
for what they are.
They made him a wastrel.

SYLPH

And we are the servants
who serve him in sorrow
for he is the son
who with tokens of sonship
came to this country.
My fruits must I offer
as long as they ripen.
With food must I feed him
and serve it in grief.

GNOME (*putting more
dishes on the table*)

We are the servants
and must still carry out
the duties of service.
But mark my words,
it cannot go on so for ever.
All is consumed and nothing created.

SYLPH

He is misguided.
They also mislead him.
How can the Father
give him unprotected into their hands?

(*The son comes in with the light and the dark devils as his
boon companions.*)

YOUNGER SON

This country is mine
for I am the Father's son.
The servants knew me at sight.

Once it was part of His realm
but He comes here no more.
He gave me my inheritance
and allowed me to depart.
At first I hardly knew where I was
but now I know my way about.
This shall be a kingdom of my own.
and I will live from its wealth.

LIGHT DEVIL

It is not yet in reality
a kingdom of your own.
But you can make it so, if you listen to me.

DARK DEVIL

There is much still to be done
to make it a land worth having.
If you listen to me, it shall be so.

YOUNGER SON

In the light of this world
there emerge to my travelling eye
such wonders above and below
wherever around me I look.
The mountains uplift their heads
to the sky spread over the Earth
where the great clouds come and go.
The moving seas stretch wide
their waters from shore to shore
and the winds press endlessly on.
Within the extent of the land,
within the expanse of the seas
are sheltered the manifold wonders
of life that has come into being
in standing stones and resting rocks,
in spreading trees and opening flowers,
in flying birds and gliding fish,
in busy insects and footed beasts.
All things seen are mine to enjoy.

(*The gnome comes in still grumbling.*)

GNOME

This wealth of wonders is kept
and tended by us, the servants,
for you who are idle and thankless.
Without us there would soon be little
still living for you to enjoy.

YOUNGER SON

You do the duty appointed

to you within the world order.
It is as it should be.
You maintain and I enjoy.

LIGHT DEVIL   When you looking see
and seeing know yourself
and the world outspread around,
that use of sense you have from me.

DARK DEVIL   When you handling touch
and touching know to be
what is about you firm and true
you have reality from me.

YOUNGER SON   Do I not possess the world
out of myself?
Am I not rich with my own treasure?

BOTH DEVILS   You are in debt to us!

YOUNGER SON   I was so rich being my Father's son
and now I am in debt.
How can this be?

LIGHT DEVIL   Your golden cloak shall be mine.
You owe it to me.

(He takes the cloak, leaving the son with only the golden stole.)

DARK DEVIL   You owe me the stars in your crown.
I shall make good use of them.

(He takes some of the stars, but they will not all come off in his hands.)

YOUNGER SON   What has become of me?
You have taken what is mine
and left me less than I was.
Take back what I have from you
and give me my own.

LIGHT DEVIL   You cannot have what you have lost.
But see, I will comfort you.
You shall have a cloak from me.

(He puts a reddish glittering cloak round the son's shoulders and embraces him.)

You shall be my dearest brother,
and share my kingdom with me.

YOUNGER SON   Am I to find new brothers?
(*puzzled*)

DARK DEVIL   I can use your stars better than you
but you shall have something from me.

(*He puts some paper stars in place of the gold ones.*)

You think paper is too poor?
Look at what is printed there.
You are getting some of my secrets.

(*He takes him by the arm and hisses in his ear.*)

You will be my crony one day,
if you know how to make good.
His kingdom is in the clouds.
You will get something solid with me.

(*The son looks frightened and draws away.*)

YOUNGER SON   How different I look,
(*looking down at himself*)   but I am not the son in my Father's house.
Here I must learn to change
and be something on my own.

(*The sylph comes in with a big dish. When she sees the son she screams and puts the dish down.*)

SYLPH   Oh fearful misery,
what has befallen you?

YOUNGER SON   Stop wailing, bring the food.
(*angry*)   My friends and I are ready for the feast.

(*The gnome comes in.*)

GNOME   What is this all about?
Glory be! What have you come to?

SYLPH   I shall be off, away,
this is no lord for me.

GNOME   Stop, we may not forget
what has been laid on us
as our duty.
This world must be maintained

as long as lasts the strength
with which we do our work.

SYLPH

Since he came, what has he given
to us of the wealth he brought?
He fritters it away himself.
Look at him now. What hope is there
for him in time to come?

GNOME

What was appointed to us
must be continued.

(*He and the sylph finish setting the table and retire.*)

YOUNGER SON

Take your seats my friends.

(*They all sit at the table.*)

The servants know their work.
What they expect from me
I never comprehend.
This world around us
gives what we can enjoy.
The experience of all it gives
is ample occupation.
It fills my soul to the brim.

LIGHT DEVIL

Fill yourself to the brim
with the wealth of this world.
In what is around and within
you will discover enough
to swell out your inner being
with the warm content of feeling
that fosters the glow of selfhood.
You will feel yourself right and good,
indulging in sympathy
with all that is filled with beauty.
But be warned.
If into this world you descend
beyond the stage of experience
you will forfeit your happiness.
You will be drawn to the interest
of what is belonging to matter.
In getting and spending,
your human nature will coarsen
and your soul that would upwards soar

will downwards sink to the depths.
Fill yourself full with all
that will enrich your selfhood,
but don't be involved with this world.
I will lead you upward and onward.

DARK DEVIL

Don't listen too much to him.
He is on bad terms with reality
and wants to lure you away.
There is more to know in this world
than you have discovered already.
I can show you the secret
of how to calculate forces
that work below the appearance.
What you grasp, you can control.
You can become the master
of its mighty mechanism
and steer the power of this world
to the ends you set yourself.
None can be your teacher but me.
Wake up from your childish state
and learn the powers of your mind.
With them control the world
and make it a place of your own.
Descend with me into reality
and become the master.

YOUNGER SON
(*looking from one to the
other*)

I met you both first in this country
and both have become my companions
but each contradicts the other
and offers the opposite counsel,
and here am I between you both.
What shall I do?

LIGHT DEVIL

Follow me to the heights
where the darkness fades
and dissolves in the distance.
The burden of your existence
shall fall away from you.

DARK DEVIL

Come with me to the depths
where you shall know the darkness
and master its powers.
You shall triumph over existence
and steer its course yourself.

YOUNGER SON	You confuse me until I cannot tell what to believe.
LIGHT DEVIL	Your pride will make you incline to me.
DARK DEVIL	Your greed will pull you towards me.
YOUNGER SON	What I have now is enough. Here is feasting in plenty. Eat and be merry with me.

(The light devil takes wine, the dark devil food, the son both.)

DARK DEVIL	Eat and feed the brain that the brain breed mind and mind masters all things.
LIGHT DEVIL	Forget him and turn to me. Drink till the winged soul soars free from solid flesh.
YOUNGER SON	Eating and drinking, tasting and feasting from all the fruits of this land there is that lacking that never before was missing. A new hunger is in me.
DARK DEVIL	Eat more.
YOUNGER SON	I cannot live by this bread only. From what did I live before?
LIGHT DEVIL	You start to hunger for the spirit.
DARK DEVIL	We must have more food. The dishes are empty. Where are the servants?
YOUNGER SON *(to light devil)*	Am I craving for the spirit?
DARK DEVIL	Spirit is empty shadow, an abstraction. You cannot feed on that. Send the servants for real food.

(The gnome and the sylph appear, carrying empty dishes, baskets.)

DARK DEVIL (*to them*)   Provide quickly.

                          (*The gnome shakes his head; the sylph wails.*)

SYLPH   No more, no more is there to bring.
                          Our strength is failing,
                          the blossoms are fading,
                          the fruit is falling,
                          the harvest has withered away.

GNOME   Our duty was done
                          while our strength has lasted,
                          but now we are starved ourselves.
                          All was consumed, nothing created
                          and famine follows.

YOUNGER SON   But where is the wealth
                          you put to use for me?
                          What has become of my inheritance?
                          I must be provided for.

GNOME   Wasted, all is wasted
                          that you brought with you.
                          You have taken all and given nothing
                          till the servants no longer
                          have power to provide.
                          Now we must leave you, thankless one,
                          to hunger and want.

YOUNGER SON   What does he mean?
                          What shall I do now?

LIGHT DEVIL   So this is the end to joy and feasting
                          that promised so well at the beginning.
                          You should have listened sooner to me.

                          (*He goes away.*)

DARK DEVIL   Hunger and want are things I can use.
                          You have no choice. You must serve me.
                          I will show you now where you belong.

                          (*He beckons and calls. Some pigs come in.*)

                          Stay here and herd pigs.

YOUNGER SON   There is no choice. What could I otherwise do?

DARK DEVIL   That fantastic brother of mine

wanted to make you a god
after his own image.
You will find your place with me,
when you learn the power of the beast
and conjure it up in yourself.

(*He goes away.*)

(*The son sits dejectedly by the pigs. He takes off the cloak
that the devil gave him and folds it up to sit on.*)

PIGS

We grub in the ground,
we rout out the roots,
we lave in the mud,
we hog up the husks.
We are exiles on Earth,
disguised in our kind
from the creatures we are
in our heavenly shape.
But in eating we still
make magic divine,
digesting base food
into forces of life.

YOUNGER SON

You are my companions now.
May I eat with you?
I am famished with hunger.

PIGS

Eat with us, if you are able.

(*They push husks towards him. Bending down to take
them his crown falls off and he tears the last portion of his
golden garment. A pig eats the paper off the crown. He
tries to eat, but throws the husks away.*)

YOUNGER SON

It is useless.
The food that the pigs can take
is empty and coarse to me.
The magic that they command
is unknown to me.
I cannot be as they.

(*He sits down with his head in his hands in despair. The
silent brother comes and stands behind him.*)

YOUNGER SON
(*to himself*)

Who am I?
What am I doing here?

What I had was not my own
but lent to me by my Father
and that has been lost.
I am reduced to what I am myself
and I am left quite alone
in a land that is not my home.
I know now what I am myself.
But what shall become of me?

(*He pauses and then continues.*)

I can recall to mind
how it is in my Father's house
under wise and loving rule.
The servants come and go
each with his duty content,
each with the bread he needs
for sustenance and life.
There is bread enough and to spare
while here I starve for food.
What the servants have and leave
would save me from perishing.

(*He pauses again. The pigs gather round but he does not notice them.*)

Once I have been the son
with his place in the Father's house.
But that can never be now
since my heritage is lost.
I left my house as a son,
as a servant I will return
and will say at once to my Father
I am unworthy of sonship
but take me into your service.
Make me one of your servants
for I cannot live without food
that will feed me with spirit-life.

PIGS (*in excitement*)	Will you go back to the Father's house? Take us with you. We also come from there and are exiles here.
YOUNGER SON	I cannot remember the way by which I was brought here. Now I must find the road

alone, with what strength I have.
It cannot fail to be hard,
lonely and full of danger.
How can I take others along
when I may fail myself?

PIGS   Do not forget us when you come home.
Come back and fetch us again
to the place, where we should be.
Remember us.

YOUNGER SON   You have been my companions here
and I will not forget you.
Farewell till some happier time.

I arise and go to my Father
on a road unknown and long,
not as a son but a beggar,
myself for what I am.
As a son I died in this country.
Shall I live again as a servant?

(*The silent brother follows him out.*)

SCENE 4

The son comes along wearily but firmly.

YOUNGER SON   Hard and steep is the road.
Sometimes I see in the distance,
shining from far beyond,
the light of my Father's house.
More often I lose altogether
sight of what lies ahead
and the weariness of the moment
smothers the sense of my purpose.
But somewhere within me
steadfastly shines the flame,
the resolve that was lit in the hour
when in sheer desolation
I came to myself.

(*The figure of the silent brother appears and passes in front of him onwards. From the side, the light devil comes to meet him.)*

LIGHT DEVIL	You have left the far country behind and have taken a course of your own. Where are you going?
YOUNGER SON	To the Father's house.
LIGHT DEVIL	In what poor shape you will appear. You departed proud as a prince, with a goodly inheritance, into a world that offered its fill of experience. Outside your Father's rule you could freely find yourself and become by right the master in a world of your own. Will you creep back a beggar?
YOUNGER SON	I have resolved to beg my Father to make me into a servant.
LIGHT DEVIL	A poor ending to a noble beginning! You are worth a better fate. You can become a prince in my world if you will acknowledge me.
YOUNGER SON	My place shall be in the Father's world. My service and my love I offer to Him, For I have grievously sinned against Him.
LIGHT DEVIL	So you refuse my over-generous help! But what of the gifts you had of me? Who will repay what belongs to me?
YOUNGER SON	They cannot be restored to you. Without them I could not make my way now. But they have been changed in use and transformed from what they were. One day you will find them anew when you seek what is yours in my Father's house.
LIGHT DEVIL	Shall I be admitted there again, I who fell from my place?
YOUNGER SON	When I see to the end of the road, the light that beckons to me

is warm with grace.

LIGHT DEVIL | When you come there, remember me.

(*He goes away. The dark devil appears from behind.*)

DARK DEVIL
(*with a sneer*)

So you are escaping at last,
a refugee from a world where you failed.
You lost a lot on this venture
with nothing to show at the end.
You should have heeded me
and things would have turned out otherwise.
But it is still not too late.
I will make you a last offer.
Take service with me and you shall inhabit
a world where everything is at your disposal;
where your will shall be
the measure of all things.

YOUNGER SON

In your world I should lose myself.
On the way to the Father's house
I find myself.

DARK DEVIL

But you are not what you are without me. Look
what I gave you.

YOUNGER SON

You gave me what I cannot do without.
But what you give
is not the same now as when you gave it.

DARK DEVIL

You are robbing me.

YOUNGER SON

If I am redeemed, your gifts will be redeemed in
me.

DARK DEVIL
(*speaking in pain*)

I am condemned to my own realm
and how shall I be released?

(*He goes away. The son begins to walk on, comforting himself with a psalm, e.g. 'I will lift up mine eyes to the hills'. He goes off and from the other side appears one of the servants of the Father on the look-out.*)

SERVANT

Again today He bade me go out and look into the
distance.
Whom does He expect?
Can He hope that one who was lost will return
again home?

(The Father appears, also looking out.)

SERVANT   There is no one in sight, sire.

FATHER   My eyes may see further than yours.

SERVANT   Do you expect him, sire, who went so long ago?

FATHER   It is more than time he came.
He must find the road hard
to be so slow coming.

SERVANT   Shall some of us go to his aid?

FATHER   That may not be.
A great helper is with him
who will speak to him
with his own voice from within.
In selfhood he shall return.
But the way is filled with dangers
and the risk will not be surmounted
until he comes within sight.

(They both look out.)

Return to the house.
Call the servants together in haste.
He is coming.

(The servant goes away. The Father moves forward and holds out His arms.)

My son, my lost son,
the one who departed and comes again,
whose life was risked and yet lives.

(The son comes in, the silent brother behind him.)

The road was long and anxious,
it has cost you so much my son
that you can hardly step to the door.
The life of your youth is exhausted
in the struggle to make the way
back from the country afar
to the place where the Father dwells.
My heart overflows with compassion
to see how the pain and the labour,
the fear and the loneliness

have put their marks upon you.

(*He embraces His son.*)

Out of the shadow of death you come
back to life.
Out of the place where you were lost
into the arms of the Father.

(*The son embraces Him now.*)

YOUNGER SON

My Father, unworthy am I
to be called again your son.
Unworthy am I to speak
with the name of Father to you.
So damaged am I by sin
who against Heaven itself
have sinned in the selfish wasting
of the manifold gifts of the Spirit
you gave me in fatherly care.
In your eyes and before your judgement
I have sinned against the Spirit
and spoilt the shape of my sonhood,
O Father, I am not worthy
to be called again your son.

FATHER (*to the two*
servants who have returned)

Call the servants together in haste;
there is much now to be done.
Fetch out the robe, the best,
the one that was laid away
for the hour of our greatest joy.

(*The servants go and return with the robe.*)

SON (*to Father*)

Let them bring the clothes of a servant;
I dare not ask for more.

SERVANTS
(*offering it to the son*)

We bring you the precious robe
woven of golden sunlight,
threaded with silver moonbeams,
crossed with the copper of Venus,
fluent with Mercury's motion,
strong with the iron of Mars,
glinting with Jupiter's tin,
weighted with Saturn's lead,
made by the great ones in chorus
who each in his moving sphere

brings forth the wealth of the heavens.
Long ago it was fashioned but never
has he been found who should wear it.

(*They put it on the son.*)

YOUNGER SON
A garment my Father gave me
when I set out from His house
into that country afar.
By my own sin I lost it,
the robe of my Father's son.
Shall I, become unworthy
to be called again His son,
inherit a robe more precious,
more princely still than the first?

FATHER (*to servants*)
Bring now the ring for his finger
that never yet has been worn.
Bring for his feet the new sandals
in which he shall walk in my realm.

YOUNGER SON
(*to Father*)
None of these gifts are deserved
that out of compassion you give.

(*Servants bring in from one side the ring, from the other
the sandals and put them on him.*)

SERVANTS
We bring you the sacred ring,
the sign of the ultimate whole.
Through one it embraces all,
embracing all it is one.
The universe gave it shape,
the Sun gave substance of gold.
The power divine within it
shall be held in your hand.

(*They put it on his finger.*)

We bring you sandals unworn
that you go with kingly step
into your Father's domain
where you shall be son and heir.
The gods who work from below
have fashioned them for your feet
to give you the gift of strength
from their world-upholding might.

(They put the sandals on his feet.)

YOUNGER SON

How can this be?
The touch of the starry robe
quickens my soul to life.
The might that flows through the ring
restores me back to my self.
The power of the shoes on my feet
gives me the courage again
to enter the Father's house.
How can I, a wastrel lost,
receive the vesture of healing
which the elder son himself
was not appointed to wear?
What does this mean?

FATHER

My son, you were lost and are found.
Your garment was spoilt and torn.
The circlet upon your head
was broken, the shoes worn out.
Now you return in need
of the forces of Heaven to heal
and renew your strength.
But from the venture you bring
one achievement wrought by yourself
out of the spirit within.
In despair you awoke to selfhood
and by its power alone
you made the perilous way
back to the house of your Father.
You bring what is here unknown,
freedom, true virtue of selfhood,
which none of the sons of God
but only he, who went out
alone to the country afar
and ventured all that he had,
could offer up to the heavens
the new force of life they need
but cannot themselves bring forth.
In the far country of Earth
the power of the future was born
when man to freedom awakes.
You were lost and are found again
Bringing the seed to selfhood.

YOUNGER SON	I saw myself as a beggar, not as one with a treasure to give. I knew myself to be starving for lack of the heavenly bread. So I came to beg.
FATHER	The beginning of freedom is loneliness and desolation. The struggle for freedom is the awakening of the self to itself. The harvest of freedom is love that seeks beyond itself. The end of freedom is resurrection for the world.
YOUNGER SON	I never knew that I set out for such an end.
FATHER	Not for yourself alone, did you go. The risk on Himself the Father took for a greater end than you could foresee. To the shadow of death He sent the son who now is born again to life. For which great rejoicing shall be made through all this house. (*To the servants.*) Make ready the feast. Bring the best in abundance. The fatted calf shall be killed today. Voices shall sing and feet shall dance and music be made for all our joy. Call those of my household to share the feast. Let them come to rejoice with me for my son, for him who was lost and is found at last, for him who was dead and returns to life. Let him be placed at the head of the feast who ventured alone to the world unknown and brought back the treasure he went to seek.

(*The servants lead the son to the doors of the house and*

*there appears the silent brother standing there to receive
him. They all go in, the Father last. Music is heard from
the background. This could be the singing of a psalm or
other suitable music. A servant or servants could do
Eurythmy or dancing outside the portico. The elder son
comes in.)*

ELDER SON

All in the fields is in order
over the stretch of lands
where I went as my Father's regent
to help with the husbandry
and remained until now.
My Father will welcome the news
of a promising harvest to come.

(A servant comes out.)

What is astir in the house?
Music? Dancing? Why then?

(To the servant.)

What is this sound of music
and of feasting within the house?

SERVANT

Today, sire, while you were gone
to the distant fields,
your brother who went from home
to a far-off country was seen
slowly approaching this place.
I saw him and would not have known,
so wasted and weary was he,
that he was the younger son.
But your Father knew him at sight
and ran in compassion to meet him.

ELDER SON

My younger brother is here?
Returning in such poor shape?

SERVANT

I heard him say of himself
that all his wealth was lost
and he an unworthy son.
But the Father gave him the robe
that no one yet had worn
and He ordered the calf to be killed,
the best of the fatlings we had.
A splendid feast is here.

Come in, sire, and share the joy
that your Father has in the son
who has come back safe and sound.

ELDER SON   You say he has wasted all
of the wealth he took away?

SERVANT   He came like a beggar home
but full of regret and grief.

ELDER SON   And for him the fatted calf?
No, I will not come in.
Go back to the feast and say
I remain outside.

(*He sits down. The servant goes and soon the Father comes out.*)

FATHER   My son, your brother is come,
he whom we mourned as lost.
He came by a weary road
and struggled sore on the way.
Come in and bid him welcome.

ELDER SON   Has he not utterly wasted
the inheritance you gave?
Shall I welcome a wastrel?

FATHER   Think how he has travelled alone
in the place of strange temptation
where the princes of evil work.
Come and rejoice with us
that he himself is saved.
Your place at the feast is empty.

ELDER SON   For him you killed the fatted calf,
for the one who wasted your wealth
and spent his all with companions,
spendthrift and frivolous.
But I, who have served you truly
and observed your rule and order
faithfully day by day,
have never been given a feast
to which I could call my friends.
Not so much as a kid was slain for me
to provide a feast in my honour;
but for him, the fatted calf was killed,

the best that we had.

FATHER
My son, you are always with me,
at my side or taking my place
on your journeys through our lands.
All that I have is likewise your own.
We are one without separation,
in mind, in heart and in will,
having all purpose in common.
But your brother from us was divided,
and walked in the ways of error
in the land beset with evil
till the shadow of death was on him.
We should give our best for the feasting
and rejoice with all our folk,
for your brother was lost and is found,
was dead and is risen to life.

(*In the portico appear the younger son and the silent brother. The younger son stays there. The silent brother walks across to the elder brother and holds out his hand.*)

SILENT BROTHER
Our brother was dead and is alive again,
was lost and is found.

(*He leads him across to the side of the younger son.*)

FATHER
For my son was dead and is alive again,
was lost and is found.

(*The music is heard again and they go into the house.*)